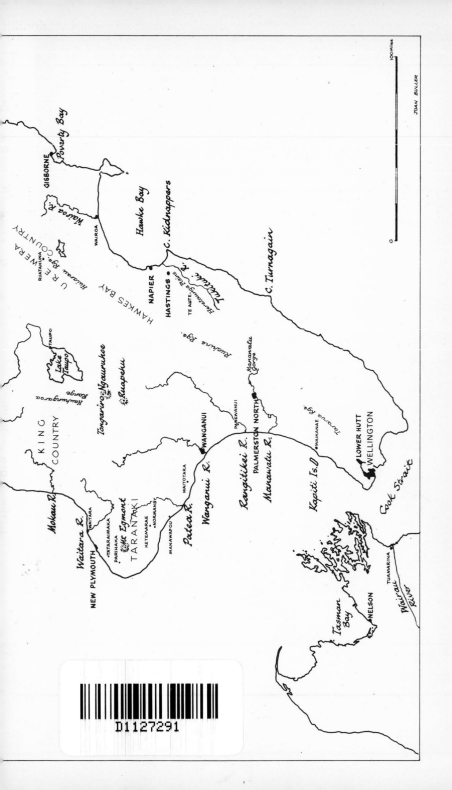

JOAN BULLER

100 Miles

GISBORNE
Poverty Bay
Wairoa R.
WAIROA
RUATAHUNA
U R E W E R A COUNTRY
Ruakituri River
HAWKES BAY
Hawke Bay
C. Kidnappers
NAPIER
HASTINGS
TE AUTE
Poukawa Lake
Tukituki R.
C. Turnagain

Lake Taupo
TAUPO
Kaimanawa Range
Tongariro Ngauruhoe
Ruapehu
Ruahine Rge.
KING COUNTRY
Mokau R.
Waitara R.
WAITARA
TATARAIMAKA
PARIHAKA
Mt. Egmont
TARANAKI
KETEMARAE
NORMANBY
MANAWAPOU
NEW PLYMOUTH
WAITOTARA
Patea R.
Wanganui R.
WANGANUI
PAREKANUI
Rangitikei R.
PALMERSTON NORTH
Manawatu R.
Manawatu Gorge
Kapiti Is.D
WAIKANAE
WAIKANAE Pa
LOWER HUTT
WELLINGTON
Cook Strait

Tasman Bay
NELSON
TUAMARINA
Wairau River

THE STORY OF THE MAORI PEOPLE

THE STORY
OF THE
MAORI PEOPLE

by

G. L. Pearce, M.A.

drawings by
Harry Dansey

Collins

AUCKLAND AND LONDON

FIRST PUBLISHED 1968
SECOND IMPRESSION 1969
THIRD IMPRESSION 1970

COLLINS BROS. & CO. LTD.

P.O. BOX NO. 1, AUCKLAND

DEDICATION

To the leaders of the Maori people who seek
inspiration from the past, goodwill in the
present and wisdom for the future, this book
is dedicated.

Type set 'Monophoto' in 12/13 pt. Bembo by
Photo Engravers Ltd, Auckland, N.Z.
PRINTED IN HONG KONG
BY DAI NIPPON PRINTING CO. (INTERNATIONAL) LTD.

Contents

Illustrations

Diagrams

Chapter decorations are all meaningful. An explanatory key will be found at the back of the book.

1

The Ancestral Homeland

UNTIL COMPARATIVELY RECENTLY the story of the Maori people could not be traced back with any degree of certainty for more than a few hundred years before it vanished into the mists of legend. Beyond the legends lay myths even more insubstantial – and that was the apparent limit of research.

Now, however, the story is very different. The painstaking work of archaeologists, the careful observations and deductions of anthropologists, and the research of linguists have established facts that were not even guessed at before and have corrected many previous misconceptions. Radiocarbon dating, too, has given us a time-scale, and not only enables us to decide conclusively that certain finds in various localities date from the same period, but has even determined their actual age within reasonably close limits.

The work is still proceeding and much is obscure even now, but the fog is lifting, landmarks are beginning to appear and the general direction of the pathway is becoming more apparent every day. We now reckon Maori history in terms

". . . the fog is lifting."

of thousands of years instead of hundreds, and can look back to the Neolithic period of South-East Asia, four thousand years ago, for our starting point.

All the evidence points to the racial origin of the Maori people as being basically Caucasian. There may well have been a slight Negroid admixture, and an even slighter infusion of Mongoloid, but the overwhelmingly dominant element is Caucasian, especially of that Mediterranean type which extends widely across Southern Asia, North Africa and Southern Europe at the present day. Nor was the fair type of North-East Europe absent in the ancestral make-up of the Maori, as could be seen in the 'urukehu', the occasional light-skinned, fair-haired Maori who have been known in New Zealand from long before the coming of the pakeha.

At some remote period, the ancestors of the Maori and those of the southern European had parted company, some to go westwards and some east, until by Neolithic times they occupied a wide belt of territory from the Atlantic to the China Sea.

Nevertheless, as far away as the British Isles, there are Kerry folk in Ireland, dark Scots of the Highlands, and thousands of people in the western parts of England and in Wales, descendants of Mediterranean settlers of perhaps five thousand years ago, who differ little in features from their distant relatives, the Maori. In Spain and in Italy the resemblance is even more marked; a Maori in a crowded street of Seville or Naples would pass unnoticed among the Spaniards or Italians around him.

To the north of the ancestral Maori in ancient times were the Mongoloid Chinese and to the south were the dark-skinned Australoids and Papuans who at that time occupied considerable areas of what are now Malaya, Indonesia and Indo-China. As may be expected, there was some admixture of races along the zones where the people of these three types were neighbours.

We must not imagine that any of these populations were

there in large numbers. It has been observed that a single family dependent entirely upon hunting or food-gathering needs a hundred square miles of territory to itself if the food-supplies are not to be too depleted to support it. All the evidence so far available indicates that the inhabitants of much of South-East Asia were at this stage in 2000 B.C.

On the coast of South China, however, there are signs of a level of culture in which primitive agriculture had begun, but the little scattered settlements were still largely dependent upon fish and shell-fish. These people were a step ahead of those further south, but their mode of life was still not far enough advanced to permit a significant increase in the density of population. Moreover, the settlements give few indications of permanence, so that presumably the inhabitants moved on when food supplies decreased.

It is along this South China coast that excavations in recent years have revealed implements showing such a marked affinity with Polynesian ones as to make it almost a certainty that this was the area in which the typical Polynesian culture originally developed. This was the first Hawaiki.

Migration because of food shortage was apparently frequent among these people, but such a situation was a strictly localised one, and it is unlikely that by itself it could have brought about the steady outward movement which obviously took place. We must look further afield for the reason, to the developing Chinese kingdom along the Hoang-ho.

The inhabitant of a flimsy hut beside the South China Sea would have known extremely little of the outside world – and cared less. He would have been completely unaware that the boundaries of the kingdom of the Shang dynasty were expanding and that Chinese settlers in increasing numbers were crossing the Yangtse-kiang to seek new homes amid the dense forests further south. But as the Chinese moved in, the original inhabitants would find that the delicate balance of adjustment to the conditions of their life was upset. Many remained where they were, changed their way of life and became absorbed into the incoming Mongoloid population. Others moved southward, setting up a chain-reaction which was to have far-reaching effects.

The Yangtse-kiang was six hundred miles away from the fisherman of the southern coast, but he was to feel the impact of the Chinese advance nevertheless. He would have become increasingly aware that more and more settlements of strangers from the north were appearing in his territory until the competition for food supplies became too intense.

He would have only two alternatives: to live in semi-starvation or to go. Behind him lay the great forests of the interior; before him lay the sea. Both were fraught with many perils, both known and unknown, but it was the sea that he knew best. Accordingly it was to the sea that he entrusted the lives of himself and his family and, taking his scanty possessions, left the familiar shore to launch out into the unknown.

There was no massive migration. Each individual family or small community had to make its own decision and those who left would have gone in small groups, but it was a movement spread over hundreds of years which was to take the men of the mainland first into the island groups festooned between Asia and Australia and eventually into and across the Pacific itself.

2

The Long Migration

THE SAILOR WHO VOYAGES along a coast needs skill in sea-
manship, but so long as he is close to shore he feels that he
has a reasonable chance of reaching safety if a storm is
approaching, especially if his craft is a small one which can
be beached without too much difficulty. He has the same
feeling of security if he is among islands where land is always
in sight.

On the other hand to venture across stretches of sea where
he finds himself with nothing but water to the horizon in all
directions makes far greater demands on him. Unless he is
fleeing in sheer desperation, he must have confidence in his
vessel and his own ability to navigate as well as the strength
of will to resist panic in the loneliness of the ocean.

Along much of the route taken by the ancestors of the
Maori people land is never far away, but there are three
water barriers between Asia and Western Polynesia each of
which in turn would provide a test of quality for both
vessels and men.

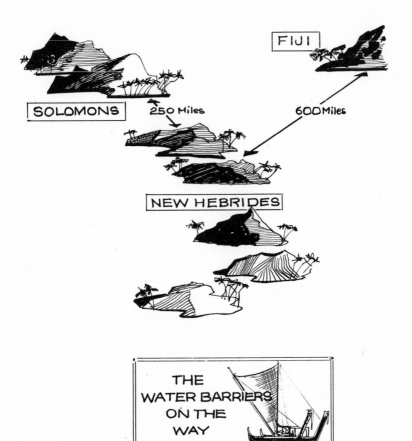

SOLOMONS

250 Miles

FIJI

600 Miles

NEW HEBRIDES

THE
WATER BARRIERS
ON THE
WAY

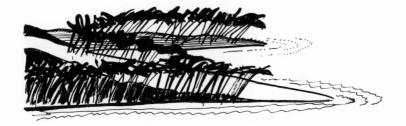

The first is between Formosa and the island of Luzon in the Philippines, three hundred miles, but with islands en route. These islands are not large and at night or in stormy conditions could easily be missed. Nevertheless, stone implements found in the Philippines show that men were living there from very remote times. Whether these first inhabitants came from the north or by the longer route through Indonesia, where the water gaps are narrower, is not known, but they certainly were there long before the Polynesian ancestors arrived.

From the Philippines to the easternmost island of the Solomons it is possible to sail for five thousand miles without losing sight of land. Then comes the next barrier – the 250 miles of open sea between San Cristoval in the Solomons and the nearest island of the Santa Cruz group to the north of the New Hebrides, followed soon afterwards by the much more formidable third barrier, the 600-mile gap between the New Hebrides and Fiji.

We know now that in the thousand years between 2000 B.C. and 1000 B.C., the ancestors of the Maori had reached as far as this third barrier and were on the point of overcoming it.

During that thousand years we may picture the islands of Melanesia and the northern shores of New Guinea as a very sparsely populated region, with small isolated communities scattered along the beaches, on off-shore islands and beside rivers in the interior jungle. Yet there apparently was sufficient contact between them to produce a certain uniformity in their way of life, based not only on the natural products of the sea and jungle but also on imported plants and animals.

The pig, the jungle fowl and the dog were undoubtedly brought from Asia; so too were the breadfruit, pandanus, yam and sugar-cane. It would be almost impossible for any of these plants or animals to survive long ocean crossings without being brought by man.

There would have been continual comings and goings

among these people for various reasons, mostly short-step migrations, but usually along the line of least resistance, towards uninhabited areas. To some extent the sea-barriers would have acted like dams across a river, causing a build-up of population and a spreading in all possible directions to the limits of navigation. This is shown by the languages of different areas of Melanesia, where islands off the main stream of migration have tended to preserve archaic forms as a result of isolation after a barrier had been passed and they had been left in a backwater.

Linguistic research has shown that there was an early division of the Malayo-Polynesian languages into a Western group, spoken by the people of Indonesia, the Philippines and far-off Madagascar, and an Eastern group to which the Melanesian and Polynesian languages belong. Apparently little contact was kept up between the migrants into Melanesia and those who remained west of New Guinea.

During the halt in the advance before the sea barrier between the New Hebrides and Fiji was overcome, isolation in the island groups of Eastern Melanesia brought about further divisions in the language. First the dialects of New Caledonia and the Loyalty group began to differentiate from those of the New Hebrides, then in the New Hebrides a division into Northern, Central and Southern languages began to appear. When the breakthrough to Fiji finally came, it was the languages of the Central New Hebrides which were taken to that country and so spread into Polynesia.

Although language relationships must not be regarded as necessarily implying physical relationships between peoples, they do at least show lengthy cultural contacts. It is clear that the Melanesian people of today are of mixed origin, in which both Polynesian and Negroid have played their part. That mingling might have taken place in Asia or Melanesia, or, as is most likely, in both regions, for the two peoples were in contact in both.

"Losing their course in a storm."

However, in all that vast expanse of ocean and jungle, with thousands of communities virtually isolated as far as inter-marriage was concerned, the laws of heredity would have been producing through the centuries a wide range of human types varying from Caucasian to Negroid, through all the possible intermediate varieties. It may have been pure chance that determined which types first settled Fiji and Tonga, or there may have been some reason which is still unknown. Nevertheless, of one fact we can be sure: it was largely brown-skinned Caucasian-type immigrants who colonised Tonga and whose descendants are the Maori of today.

As each of the major sea barriers was reached, the eastward movement would have come to a halt until the spirit of adventure or the force of necessity impelled families again to venture far out into the unknown. It was not that the migrants were unable to cross the wide stretch of sea in most cases, but simply that, as long as suitable settlement areas were available closer at hand, there was no incentive to go further afield for a new home. Undoubtedly there were many accidental drift-voyages, usually with only men in the canoes, but the call of home is strong and people who had been carried unintentionally to an unknown and unin-habited island through losing their course in a storm would rarely choose to remain.

They were capable navigators with a detailed knowledge of the stars and whenever the skies were clear they would have been in no doubt as to their latitude, even though longitude could not be calculated.

No deliberate attempt at new settlement beyond a wide expanse of water would have been made unless the voyagers had confidence in the craft on which they embarked, but that confidence was fully justified. The double canoe, which had been used in South-East Asian waters for hundreds of years and was the major deep-sea vessel of Melanesians and Poly-nesians is a most seaworthy craft. It is difficult to overturn and is almost unsinkable; with a large steering oar it can sail

to within 45 degrees of the wind, and under average conditions can travel at least 120 miles a day.

Finally the decisive step was taken and first Fiji and then
Tonga received their first permanent settlers; the archaeological record indicates that this took place shortly after
1000 B.C.

3
The People of Tangaroa

SO FAR WE HAVE NOT BEEN ABLE to speak of any particular
leader among these ancestors of the Maori, for personal
names have not survived from those remote times, but with
the migration out of Melanesia it is possible at last to refer
to two who in all probability took a leading part in the
voyaging of those days.

In early religions throughout the world it is very common
for famous ancestors to be held in such respect that eventually
they come to be worshipped as gods; the same deification of
outstanding leaders took place among the Polynesians.

Most of the Maori gods appear in the ancient religions of
Eastern Polynesia, but there is only one, Tangaroa, who was
known further west. Tangaroa was widely worshipped as
the god of the sea, of seafarers and fishermen. In Samoa and
Tonga, as in some of the islands to the east he was the supreme
god. The Samoans claimed that he created their islands, and
his worship was centred on the island of Tau in the Manua
group. In the New Hebrides too, as Tangaro, he was chief of

the gods; yet in the nearby Banks Islands he was regarded as a power of evil forever attempting to overthrow any good that his elder brother, Qat, might do.

It would be useless to try to find a literal meaning in all the imaginative poetry of myths; yet there are often hard facts on which the myths are based. When we look for the basic truths in the myths of Tangaroa, the story below is probably not far from the truth: Tangaroa was the restless younger son of a chief on the Banks Islands. After a long and bitter quarrel with his older brother, after the latter had succeeded to the chieftainship, which clearly made a very deep impression on the people of the island, he was either driven out or left of his own free will to establish a colony in the New Hebrides. It was there that he became a powerful chief, and having led his followers on to Tonga, and voyaged far and wide, he finally settled on Tau in the Samoan islands which he had discovered. He had established his reputation as such an outstanding navigator and explorer that centuries later he was numbered among the gods.

Those were heroic days, and still another well-known name in Maori mythology was probably also a great navigator of the past. Legends of the marvellous adventures of Maui are widespread but, although held in great esteem, he was apparently not worshipped as a god except by the Tongans who claimed that he had fished their islands up from the sea. He is credited with having fished up numerous islands in different parts of Polynesia, but it seems most likely that the tale of his fishing prowess originated in Tonga, and was later transferred to islands elsewhere. It is feasible that Maui in real life was the navigator who discovered Tonga, and perhaps other islands, but was possibly not of high rank, ·so that he failed to achieve deification at a later date except in his own colony of Tonga.

Myths and legends have clustered thickly round both Tangaroa and Maui, but in spite of the aura of divinity the personalities of the men show through. The ancient Poly-

Tangaroa, god of the sea.

nesians honoured their memory in the highest manner that they knew; we can still accord them respect as able leaders of men.

Apart from the fact that there is open ocean for hundreds of miles to eastward of Fiji, Tonga and Samoa, those islands comprise a large area, so that it is not surprising that it was several hundred years before a further move was made to the east.

Yet when that move did come, the voyagers travelled far, for the Marquesas were the next islands to be settled. Tahiti received its first colonists at about the same time. Excavations in both indicate that their culture was definitely from Western Polynesia, and the earliest finds date from about 200 B.C.

Once again came a pause for development. Villages grew larger, more and more land came into cultivation and methods of agriculture improved as they became adjusted to local conditions. The pioneer days of small settlements, where all were forced to produce food in order to survive, slowly gave place to tribal organisation with distinct social classes and an aristocracy of hereditary chiefs.

Religion developed into an elaborate system of worship under the guidance of the priest, the tohunga whose spiritual authority and mana was at least equal to the political authority of the rangatira.

The ritual ceremonies of the tohunga took place on the marae, some of which in later years were most imposing structures. A wall surrounded an open courtyard with a raised stone platform, the ahu, at one end; sometimes platform was built upon platform, forming a series of stone steps leading to the upper terrace on which the sacred rites were performed. At the famous Taputaputea marae in Raiatea, erected after the last Maori migration to New Zealand, the ahu was 141 feet long and was raised twelve feet above the ground.

The impressiveness of the marae afforded an indication

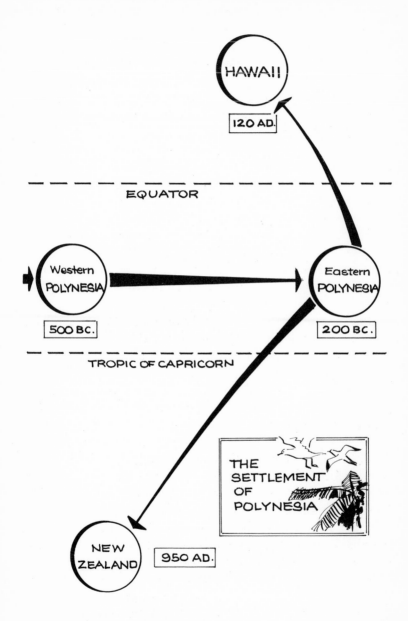

HAWAII

120 AD.

EQUATOR

Western POLYNESIA

500 BC.

Eastern POLYNESIA

200 BC.

TROPIC OF CAPRICORN

THE
SETTLEMENT
OF
POLYNESIA

NEW ZEALAND

950 AD.

of the prosperity of a community which was so far removed from bare subsistence agriculture as to be able to devote much time to non-productive work.

The four chief gods that were eventually worshipped in Eastern Polynesia were Tangaroa, Tane, Rongo and Tu. It is reasonable to suppose that the last three were originally outstanding leaders in the early days whose personality had so impressed their followers that their memory was kept green by raising them to divine status. Tane was the ruler of the forest, Rongo presided over peace and agriculture, and Tu was the god of war.

As the population increased, so the causes of migration in the past again began to appear. The traditions speak repeatedly of migrants fleeing from enemies, or leaving islands which were over-populated or suffering from famine. Banishment for offences against tribal law, too, was not uncommon as social organisation became more highly developed.

But, despite all these enforced voyages, whether short or long, we must not lose sight of the fact that the Polynesians are a seafaring people in whom is a strong love of adventure and an urge to travel for the sake of travel itself.

About 200 A.D. the islands of Hawaii were colonised from Tahiti, and remote Easter Island was probably settled by Marquesans about two hundred years later. Other islands, previously unknown or at least uninhabited, became little outposts of Polynesian culture, but although lengthy voyages were being undertaken, it was not until between 950 and 1000 A.D. that we can be sure that the first Maoris reached New Zealand, the largest islands of the Polynesian world.

There are hints in ancient legends that some navigators may have come at least as far south as New Zealand before that date, but there is no real proof of it.

In the story of Ui-te-Rangiora, he is said to have seen what have been interpreted as ice-bergs. This need not necessarily imply a visit to Antarctic waters, for there is an

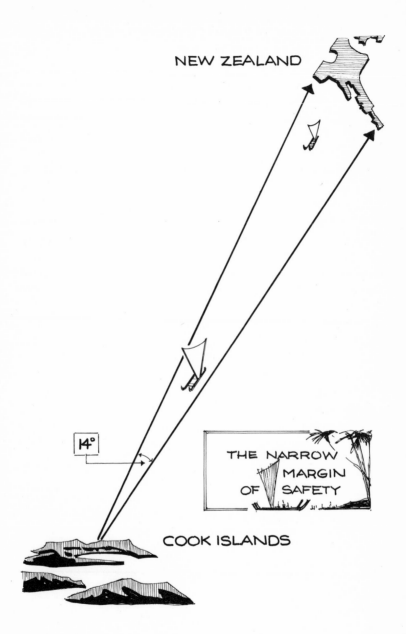

NEW ZEALAND

14°

THE NARROW
MARGIN
OF SAFETY

COOK ISLANDS

area of the ocean, east of the Chatham Islands, where floating ice is often sighted, in the same latitude as Wellington. It is recounted that another chief, Aru-tanga-nuku, was inspired by Ui-te-Rangiora's tale to set sail southward to see the wonders for himself.

Kupe is the man to whom the discovery of New Zealand is attributed in Maori legend, and, despite miraculous and improbable additions to the story, there is no real reason to doubt his voyage. Nevertheless evidence is accumulating that the first settlers had arrived before Kupe; certain recent finds suggest a date up to more than 200 years earlier.

By calculation from genealogies, Kupe's voyage has been dated at about 925 A.D., which accords satisfactorily with archaeological evidence. Although Kupe himself is said to have returned to Hawaiki and never revisited New Zealand, it is clear that it was about that time that an influx of Polynesians occurred, and a new era in Maori history began.

4
South to Aotea-roa

THERE IS THEREFORE EVIDENCE that there was settlement in New Zealand at about the time of Kupe's voyage and continued sporadically for several centuries. In the South Island the name of Rakaihautu was remembered as the discoverer of the country and leader of the first settlers.

Those who arrived in the first hundred years or so would have left Tahiti before the social developments already mentioned had begun to approach their peak, but even with later arrivals there is a complete absence of the temple-building that became characteristic of the longer-settled islands of Eastern Polynesia. This is not surprising, for such a culture is the mark of a mature, prosperous and economically secure community, whereas in New Zealand the settlers were in the pioneer stage, with small numbers of people scattered over wide territories.

The climate and the natural resources of the country were so totally different from what they had been accustomed to that the early Maoris had to readjust their whole way of life. There is little indication that food plants, even if they were introduced from the north, ever became firmly established in these early centuries. If the settlers brought fowls and pigs, these did not survive; only the kuri, the Polynesian dog, has left its bones to be found by excavators in the ancient settlements. Perhaps any form of agriculture or keeping of domestic animals and birds was considered unnecessary in a country so richly endowed with food that could be obtained readily by the fisherman or the hunter.

Moas were plentiful and not difficult to hunt down. As a consequence, the economy of these people for centuries was based on the moa. But the life of the hunter does not lead to the formation of large communities in which the interplay of ideas brings progress. The culture of the Moa-Hunters tended to remain unchanged while, unknown to them, the rest of the Pacific world was leaving them behind.

Although the known Moa-Hunter camp-sites are chiefly on the east coast of the South Island, some have been found further north even as far as Mt Camel, Houhora, in Northland and there is good reason to believe that many others will come to light in different parts of the country. As may be expected with such a sparse population, no fortified villages have been found, and weapons are conspicuously absent.

According to tradition the people of the Chatham Islands were descended from Rongomai-whenua, a contemporary of Kupe; there are frequent references to the arrival of canoes from New Zealand. The place-names of the Chathams show certain affinities with those of the Waitaki area of the South Island, a region well-known for its signs of Moa-Hunter occupation.

Immigrants continued to arrive in New Zealand, but were absorbed into the population without apparently altering the general way of life. Three chiefs whose names have been remembered among the later arrivals were Toi and Whatonga, who can be dated at about 1150 A.D., and Manaia, perhaps two centuries later.

The population grew steadily larger – but a change was beginning to make itself felt. The moa was nearing extinction. Finally it disappeared completely from coastal areas and, although hunters pushed further inland than before in search of their prey, the majority of the people were forced to turn to other sources of supply for their food. It is not easy to discover just how long the last few surviving moas remained but, although moa-hunting appears to have ended in the North Island two centuries earlier, it possibly continued in remote areas of the South Island until 1550 at the latest.

There is very little recorded in the traditions about any tribal groupings among the early Moa-Hunters. It is said that one early body of settlers who landed in Taranaki eventually divided into four tribes, the Tini-o-Maruiwi who occupied the Auckland isthmus, the Tini-o-Ruatamore in Northland, the Tini-o-Taitawaro who remained in North Taranaki, and the Tini-o-Pananehu.

Twenty-two tribal names from the time of Toi and Whatonga have been remembered, but none have survived as names of recent tribes.

About 1350 came the last known immigration from Polynesia, the arrival of the canoes known as the Fleet. It brought in no large numbers of settlers, yet its influence was far-reaching.

Conquest of the local inhabitants by the handful of new arrivals was out of the question, yet in a very short time we find that the descendants of the Fleet Maoris had become dominant in almost all the major tribes of the country. There is no doubt that the secret of their successful bid for power lay in their possession of food plants, chief of which was the kumara. The taro and yam were also brought, but their use was very limited, whereas the kumara was rapidly spread throughout the North Island and the northern parts of the South Island.

The traditions of almost all the canoes speak of warfare before their departure; in many cases the voyage was a flight from a too powerful enemy. With the population of Raiatea and Tahiti increasing rapidly, the possession of food plantations had become a prestige symbol of which chiefs were extremely jealous. Produce rent was paid by sub-chiefs to chiefs from whom they leased their land, and conflict over the amount paid was apparently common. Several tales tell of Maori ancestors incurring the enmity of a certain Uenuku the ariki, a powerful high chief in Hawaiki at that time.

The canoes of the Fleet did not necessarily leave together, but all seem to have arrived within a few years of each other, and a period of rapid development ensued. Within a generation the conservative and static culture of the Moa-Hunter tribes of the North Island was stirred into new life by the dynamic new-comers. The former ruling class was superseded and their traditions faded away from human memory.

So complete was the erasure of the past that, until recently, Maori history in New Zealand was regarded as beginning with the Fleet, and the earlier inhabitants were so despised by the new families of chiefs that the descriptions of them led to the belief that they belonged to some primitive race and were not Polynesians at all. Toi was considered to be a Maori, but the impression created was that his colony was a lone Polynesian group doomed to be eventually absorbed into the inferior population around it.

We know now that this picture is completely false and that the Moa-Hunters were the ancestors of the present-day Maori people.

Seven canoes are usually recognised as having belonged to the Fleet: Tainui, Te Arawa, Mataatua, Kurahaupo, Tokomaru, Aotea and Takitimu. The story of each is well known, as also are the names of their commanders and their descendants. Although at first only the aristocracy would have been able to prove Fleet ancestry, it is clear that after six centuries of intermarriage such a claim can rightly be made by all in the tribe. This is illustrated by the fact that whereas the names of the actual canoe immigrants show

The seven canoes.

little affinity with New Zealand place-names, those of later generations are clearly similar in type to names previously established here.

Several other canoes are mentioned in tradition, the genealogies indicating that they came as part of the same general movement, although probably slightly earlier, and in view of the importance in Maori life of descent from particular canoes, they are included in the list below.

Canoe	Commander	Chief Tribes	District
Tainui	Hoturoa	Waikato Ngatimaniopoto Ngati Haua Ngati Maru Ngati Paoa Ngati Raukawa Ngati Toa Ngaitai	From Tamaki to the King Country including Coromandel
Te Arawa	Tamatekapua	Te Arawa federation Ngati Tuwharetoa	Bay of Plenty coast at Maketu to south of Lake Taupo
Mataatua	Toroa	Ngati Awa Tuhoe Whakatohea Whanau a Apanui	Eastern Bay of Plenty and Urewera
Kurahaupo	Maungaroa (Taranaki version)	Taranaki	Taranaki
	Ruatea (Wanganui version)	Atihau Ngati Apa Rangitane Muaupoko	Wanganui south to Cook Strait
		Te Aupouri Te Rarawa	Far North
Tokomaru	Whata	Ngati Tama Ngati Mutunga Ngati Rahiri Manukorihi Puketapu Atiawa Ngati Maru	North and Central Taranaki
Aotea	Turi	Ngati Ruanui Ngarauru Atihau	South Taranaki Wanganui
Takitimu	Tamatea	Rongowhakaata Ngati Kahungunu Ngaitahu	East coast of North Island south from Poverty Bay. Also South Island

Canoe	Commander	Chief Kribes	District
Horouta	Pawa	Ngatiporou	East Coast north of Poverty Bay
Mamari	Nukutawhiti	Ngapuhi Te Rarawa Aupouri	Far north to Kaipara
Mahuhu	Rongomai	Ngati Whatua	Kaipara to Tamaki

After the social revolution at the time of the Fleet, the governing factors of the climate, the build of the country and the fertility of the soil would have largely determined the distribution of the population which is unlikely to have been very different four or five hundred years ago from what it was at the time of the arrival of the pakeha, although of course the actual numbers would have been less.

More than four-fifths of the people were living in the northern region, the area of extensive cultivation on the lowlands extending from the far north to the Waikato basin and continuing round the coasts to the Wanganui River on the west and the Heretaunga Plains on the east. In the rest of the North Island and along the South Island coast from Tasman Bay to just south of Banks Peninsula, the region in which most of the remainder lived, agriculture was far less important.

Finally, possibly only about 3 per cent were scattered over the greater part of the South Island, a semi-nomad backward people largely dependant on sea food and having little contact with the northern tribes except to barter their products of greenstone and mutton-birds.

In the political organisation of the Maori people, the iwi (tribe) took first place. Tribes which had grown too large for effective control might subdivide into hapu (sub-tribes), but, although hapu did not necessarily remain friendly and quarrels on occasion became bitter, if danger threatened from another tribe, tribal loyalty outweighed all other considerations. The link between tribes descended from arrivals on the same waka (canoe) was weaker, but nevertheless could be invoked in a last appeal for help from a reluctant chief.

Loyalty to the tribe involved personal loyalty to the rangatira, the chief who held his position by right of birth. The eldest son succeeded his father as rangatira, and where a tribe had subdivided the eldest son in the senior family held the highest rank as ariki among the rangatira.

When the eldest child of an ariki was a daughter, she was treated with the greatest respect, but it was extremely rare for her to succeed to the active leadership of the tribe. The mana of the ariki symbolised the power and prestige of the tribe but, in addition, through his descent he acquired a personal tapu and was regarded by his people with the awe of something mysterious and divine.

Below the hereditary aristocracy were the tutua, all other free members of the tribe; and on the lowest grade in the social structure were the taurekareka, slaves captured in war, who had no rights and only such privileges as their captors might permit.

The tribe was the unit, not only in political matters but in almost every aspect of life. Maori society was built firmly on the basis of the rights and responsibilities of the community. The ariki spoke for his tribe; the community profited from the labours of the individual and took responsibility for his misdeeds; his successes or misfortunes were shared by all.

Although a man's right to the sole use of any form of personal property was freely recognised and could be inherited, his ownership was never absolute. One most important application of these communal rights was in the ownership of land. Each individual, as a member of the tribe, shared in the ownership of the tribal land. Whatever land was apportioned out to him was granted with the right of use only, and what is not owned cannot be sold.

The right of the tribe to own land was based on one of three claims: ancestral inheritance, conquest or cession. Right of conquest was not valid unless the conquerors not only occupied the land but also ensured that none of the former inhabitants remained. Cession of land was rare and usually was the result of an agreement whereby a tribe recognised a fault committed by one of its members and handed over land as compensation.

The existence of right of conquest meant, of course, that no land could be securely held unless the tribe was powerful enough to defend it against aggression, and there is ample evidence that, especially in the earlier centuries after the Fleet, wars of expansion were not uncommon. As time went on, and ancestral claims to land became stabilised, tribes rarely seized land; but the growing prestige of tribes and their chiefs often led to war to avenge insult, either deliberate or unintentional.

The irresponsible or guilty act of an individual could bring tragedy to his tribe, for the whole community was held to be collectively responsible for what had happened. Moreover, a feud in which the death of one man could only be avenged by the death of a member of the tribe responsible could continue generation after generation without an end. The law of utu (recompense) was inflexible.

Where the ancestral land of two powerful tribes adjoined, there was always the risk of a local quarrel flaring into a tribal war. It is no wonder that a tremendous amount of work went into the construction of hill-top pas with strong defences, when defence was essential for survival.

However, despite the constant recurrence of tales of warfare in Maori traditions, it must not be assumed that war occupied their whole life. The arts of peace flourished, too. New techniques in mat-weaving were developed as Pacific island methods were found unsuitable when used with flax. The need for warmer clothing in the New Zealand climate led to the development of the simple rain-cape into a full-length cloak in which one remarkable innovation was the fitting of the garment to the body by introducing short extra rows of weaving where required. New methods of decoration were evolved and weaving became a highly specialised art along distinctive Maori lines.

In house-building, the climate and the availability of large trees such as totara, which was relatively easy to work and resistant to rot, brought about revolutionary changes in technique.

The Maori of the olden time became a highly efficient craftsman within the limits of the tools and materials available to him. There is scarcely a joint used by present-day joiners and carpenters which was not known and employed by him over two hundred years ago.

The new type of structure, too, with wide boards, gave scope for decorative painting of interior woodwork, which advanced far beyond that of the rest of Polynesia. But it also gave excellent opportunities for the art of the carver, and it was in carving that perhaps the most spectacular changes took place. We do not know what brought about the change from the straight-line decorative carving in the islands to the involved curvilinear Maori designs, but the result is a triumph of patience, artistic sense and outstanding skill.

The work of the builder, the painter and the carver reaches its culmination in the whare whakairo (carved meeting-houses) of which the tribes are justly proud.

Experts in all branches of knowledge, including carving, were known as tohunga, but the term is perhaps better known as applied to priests, who had a special place in the community. They were educated for the position, and although ventriloquism and hypnotism were used to create supernatural awe, they undoubtedly were men of marked ability whose knowledge and wisdom in practical matters were of high value to their tribes.

Religion in New Zealand did not follow the same lines as in the other Pacific islands. The marae was separated from the ahu and became the meeting place for non-religious gatherings; no attempt was made at elaborate temple-building at the ahu which was often little more than one or two upright stones, a small cairn of rocks or even a post. It was usually well away from the village and was visited rarely, except by the priest. Organised religion as such had little part in the general life of the Maori, and although incantations asking divine protection or success in an undertaking, and special rituals on particular occasions, were a normal feature of life, the Maori attitude towards religion was essentially a practical one.

This then was the structure of Maori society which had been evolving in response to the challenge of the environment for four hundred years without contact with the outside world.

On 9 October 1769 Captain Cook landed at Poverty Bay. Tasman's visit over a century before was known to only a handful of Maoris in a remote part of the South Island and there is no evidence that it was ever heard of elsewhere. Cook, however, went ashore in several districts along the coast of the most densely settled regions of New Zealand. The news of the strange visitors spread far and wide and Maori isolation was shattered for ever.

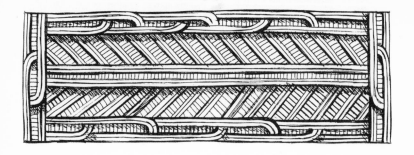

5
First Contacts with the Pakeha

THE PEOPLE OF POVERTY BAY were the first Maoris to see pakehas – and that first meeting ended in bloodshed.

Captain Cook and some of his men had gone ashore towards a few houses near the beach, leaving a guard on the ship's boat. While he was away, a group of armed Maoris approached the boat brandishing their weapons and, fearing attack, the coxswain in charge fired two shots over their heads; then, as that did not make them halt, he shot a man dead. The Maoris fled in dismay.

We cannot be sure of the exact details now. The Maori demonstration may have been a show of strength intended to warn off the strangers or perhaps it was meant simply as a ceremonial challenge. Both parties would have been highly tensed and apprehensive, and neither knew the language of the other.

To the Maori the whole encounter was almost incredible: the strange vessel, the equally strange men and their mysterious power that could strike a man dead from far away left him bewildered. The pakeha's actions were unpredictable; he appeared to be completely ignorant of the code of custom which regulated normal life. It is no wonder that there were misunderstandings, and that those misunderstandings could have violent consequences.

Cook himself was a humane man. He was recognised as a powerful chief and his relationship with Maori chiefs was almost invariably friendly, but among both Maori and pakeha of lower rank there were some whose actions caused offence and justly provoked the anger of their chiefs – those who tried to cheat in bartering goods, the Maori who stole what he coveted from the ship, the sailor who broke down fences and raided kumara plantations.

In many cases where Cook's reception was unfriendly, there was good reason for it. At Mercury Bay, where he stayed for eleven days, the Maori attitude at first was extremely hostile but an old chief who came aboard explained that his people had suffered repeatedly from Ngapuhi raids and had become suspicious of all strangers.

When the situation at the time is considered, it says much for the forbearance of both Cook and the chiefs whom he met during the course of his stay in New Zealand that this first impact of a foreign culture produced so little violence. Unfortunately that spirit of mutual toleration did not endure, and for two generations and more the harsh edges of an alien civilisation and the resistant but slowly crumbling indigenous one were grinding inexorably against each other. It was a situation which brought out the worst in both Maori and pakeha, and was equally shameful to both.

Many pakehas ignored Maori custom, violated tapu, insulted chiefs and pursued their own ends with fraud and brutality, knowing well that they were beyond the reach of European law. Maoris, dazzled by the material possessions of the pakeha, were equally fraudulent in their dealings, and even more savage in their violence.

When, in 1809, the ship *Boyd* was seized by treachery in

Whangaroa harbour and most of those aboard were killed, there was ample justification under Maori custom. A chief who had been one of the crew aboard the vessel had received a flogging by order of the captain, an unpardonable indignity for one of high rank; the Maoris of his tribe were following the normal course of utu. There were other cases, too, where an infringement of tapu led to massacre of pakehas, again a normal reaction in Maori life. But Maori custom was no excuse for some of the later unprovoked attacks on ships in which the only motive appears to have been sheer brutal greed.

Cannibalism almost invariably followed massacre and roused widespread horror in the pakeha world but it must be remembered that, in this matter, emotional reactions are conditioned by the attitude of the community. The custom had been long established among the later Maori people, although as far as is known it was not practised by the Moa-Hunters.

The main reasons for it appear to have been: firstly, the symbolic humiliation of a defeated enemy in order to gain personal prestige; and secondly, the purely material one that, in a country where meat was difficult to obtain, it was wasteful to throw away good food. Defeated enemies and slaves had no human rights whatever; their position was exactly the same as that of domestic animals today, so that the Maori had no qualms at all about eating such food.

By 1820 a new generation of Maoris had grown in knowledge of the pakeha and his ways – a cynical generation which tolerated the pakeha, not because of what he was, for there was little to admire in the riff-raff that came ashore, but for reason of what could be bought or stolen from him. Nor was that mercenary policy confined to people of common rank; chiefs realised the power that could be theirs if they had steel weapons and muskets, and when traders began to barter for dressed flax, the chiefs used their authority over their people to produce more and still more of that commodity to exchange for the coveted weapons.

The effect on the Maori of this demand for flax was disastrous. They left their villages on the hills to live beside the flax swamps in unhealthy hovels which became hot-beds of disease. The ancient Maori had been extraordinarily free from illness, and epidemics were unknown. But that same absence of disease left him without immunity and introduced diseases of little danger to the pakeha, whose resistance had been built up through the centuries, were disastrous to the Maori. Physical and mental deterioration, too, through excess of liquor, which the Maori had not known before, increased still more his susceptibility to disease.

Faced with the new problem of infamiliar illnesses, the tohunga, whose remedies in the past had helped the body to a cure or at least had done no harm, now found himself powerless. His treatments frequently aggravated the disease, and the growing lack of confidence of his people weakened the efficacy of the psychological influence on which he had formerly relied.

The chief kept his power through his right of birth and his leadership in material matters; the tohunga's power was of the mind. It is no wonder that the tohunga so often held themselves aloof in proud resentment from the pakeha who not only actively but often merely by his continued presence was undermining their previously unchallenged authority.

On the positive side it should be noted that the outlook of the Maori people had widened considerably through contact with the outside world. Young Maoris were kid-napped or went of their own free will to serve as seamen on visiting ships and travelled widely before their return; new skills were acquired and the old ones improved with pakeha tools. The value of pigs was realised from the time when Captain Cook left some among the tribes, and a taste for pork was quickly established. In the plantations, maize, pumpkins, potatoes and other vegetables were being grown to supplement the traditional diet. But one disastrous legacy of the past remained. Tribal wars which had been smouldering and flaring up at intervals for centuries began to intensify near the turn of the century.

Sometimes the spark that set them off could be directly attributed to the pakeha, as when Maoris kidnapped by ships' crews were put ashore callously among hostile tribes who promptly killed or enslaved them. In other cases, the cause was indirect and traceable rather to the general unsettling effect of pakeha contact; the presence of strangers whose weapons had such power moved chiefs subconsciously to assert their own prestige through conquests. Again, some of the conflicts would have come in any case, for the Maori world was never really at peace.

Hongi Hika and his relative, Te Morenga, of the Ngapuhi had already made their names feared among the Coromandel and Bay of Plenty tribes when Hongi conceived the scheme of making his tribe invincible by arming them with muskets on a scale unheard of previously. In 1820 he was able to visit England where his dignity so impressed George IV and others who little suspected his plans that they showered him with valuable presents. In Sydney, all but a suit of armour was exchanged for hundreds of muskets, and Ngapuhi began the campaigns that were to last for eight horrifying years.

Ngatiwhatua, Waikato, Ngatimaru and Arawa were overwhelmed in merciless slaughter, until at last even the Ngapuhi warriors themselves became weary of war, and with the death of Hongi from a musket wound received in a minor conflict at Whangaroa his tribe abandoned its bloodthirsty course.

About the same time as Hongi's visit to England, Te Rauparaha, chief of the Ngatitoa tribe at Kawhia, which was dangerously close to the powerful Waikatos, decided on the bold move of migrating with his people to a less confined region. In alliance with Ngatiraukawa, who were impelled by the same motives, the Ngatitoa warriors moved south-

Tu, the ancient war god, and Rongo, the god of peace.

ward, fighting their way through whenever they were opposed, until they reached the Wellington west coast where, after a determined resistance, the local tribes were subjugated and Te Rauparaha's base was established on Kapiti Island. Following Hongi's example, Te Rauparaha obtained muskets and carried out devastating raids which by 1837 left him in control of much of the South Island.

Tribal warfare had reached unprecedented heights of slaughter and, with the results of catastrophic wars added to the havoc of epidemics and deterioration through liquor, it appeared to observers that the Maori people were doing their best to hasten their own inevitable extinction.

But in the midst of these chaotic upheavals when Tu, the ancient war-god, seemed supreme, the Maori had not been abandoned for ever by Rongo, the god of peace. From the pakeha had come the means of self-destruction; but men of goodwill among the pakeha were to make amends. The missionaries' words of peace would at last reach the ears of men above the tumult of the warring tribes.

On 22 December 1814 Samuel Marsden arrived at the Bay of Islands in the brig *Active* from Sydney, and on Christmas Day he preached his first sermon to a Maori congregation.

It was significant that his first missionaries were a carpenter, a shoe-maker acquainted with rope-making and a school-teacher; and that he brought with him horses and cattle; for Marsden's aim was the realistic one of introducing Christianity against a background of pakeha civilisation. The mission station was to be an oasis of ordered Christian life which, by its contrast with the unsettled conditions else-where, would inspire the Maoris to follow its example.

It was several years before the missionaries made actual converts, for they were stringent in their insistence on genuine repentance and a real understanding of Christianity before they would baptise Maoris, but during those years their prestige among the people grew steadily. Repentance was a real problem for thoughtful Maoris, for a clash of cultures was involved. Many of the older people felt that, however much they respected the missionaries and their teachings, they were being asked to affirm repentance for actions and attitudes of mind which were part of the code of their ancestors.

They were not prepared to take a step which they considered to be a positive break with ancient traditions; nevertheless they remained firm friends of the missionaries and encouraged the younger generation, in whom those traditions were growing weaker, to follow Christianity.

The Ngapuhi chiefs, Hongi Hika, Korokoro and Ruatara, had taken a leading part in welcoming Marsden and staunchly supported the mission – even though Hongi's later career was far from peaceful.

In 1829 Taiwhanga, one of Hongi's fighting chiefs, was christened with the name of Rawiri (David), an appropriate name which did not replace his previous name but was added to it, and many other converts followed the same course. What the two names signified to the Maori people was that the convert, although now a Christian, was still one of his own people.

Especially in Northland, Christian Maoris were proud to receive the names of the missionaries who devoted their lives to help them, and in addition the Bible was an almost inexhaustible source upon which they could draw. Most of these names have survived as surnames to the present day. The missionary names of Selwyn, Williams, Taylor and Maunsell are still very frequent among Maoris, sometimes in their pakeha form and sometimes in Maori as Herewini, Wiremu, Teira and Manihera.

The countryside surrounding the Northland mission stations began to take on a new aspect as the missionaries succeeded in their aim of transplanting the good and useful features of English life to New Zealand. Orchards and gardens flourished, wheat and barley provided grain for the mill, and the Maori people learnt the skills of the village craftsmen of England.

It was an important step forward when Maori converts made the first move to carry Christianity to their own people, especially so when it involved going among other tribes, most of whom were bitter enemies of Ngapuhi. But the courage of the Ngapuhi warrior was transmuted into the perhaps greater courage of the Ngapuhi preacher who fearlessly risked his life for the new doctrine of peace.

Prepared to suffer death, if necessary, with the spirit of the martyrs, the sons of fighting chiefs went boldly ahead and, possibly to their own amazement, found that they were well received. Their way had often been made clearer by slaves converted to Christianity and freed by their captors under missionary influence, who had returned to their own people filled with enthusiasm for the new religion. The Bible was known to the Maori, not only from the words of the missionaries but also from his own reading, for in the mission schools the elements of education were being taught. The Maori learnt to read and write not only in English but also in his own language.

In 1820 a grammar of the Maori language with a vocabulary of a hundred pages was published by the Church of England Missionary Society and the present system of Maori spelling was established. Twenty-four years later William Williams, then Archdeacon of Waiapu, published the first edition of his famous *Dictionary of the Maori Language*, printed by the Mission Press at Paihia. That work, revised and added to by other members of the same family for over a century, is still the standard dictionary of the language.

In 1822 the Wesleyan Methodists founded a mission station at Hokianga, and were followed sixteen years later by the Roman Catholics. Each of the missions was active in sending out both pakehas and Maori converts to carry Christianity throughout New Zealand, following in canoes or on foot the old communication routes along which for centuries the Maori people had travelled in trade or war.

The main highway to the south went from Hokianga to the present site of Dargaville; from there canoes went across the Kaipara and as far as possible by water until the nearest point to the Waitemata was reached. From the Waitemata by either the Whau or the Otahuhu portage, canoes were carried to the Manukau and from that harbour another portage at Waiuku led to the Waikato, which with its tributary the Waipa was an important highway. Two tracks led from the Waipa River to Kawhia, and from there the beach was followed right to the site of Wellington. If the traveller chose to follow the Waipa River further upstream, there was a comparatively short portage to the Mokau River from Te Kuiti, and a journey with the current to the coast.

The Wanganui River was another important line of communication from which there were several links to east and west with the coastal route and with Taupo, where routes branched out to the Wairoa, the Rangitikei, the Waikato and the Bay of Plenty coast at Maketu. A track traversed the Tararuas, another went through the Manawatu gorge to where Napier now stands, and routes led from Whakatane to Gisborne and to Ruatahuna. Several branch routes crossed Taranaki. From the far north to Cape Runaway, canoes were passing constantly along the north-east coast.

On 4 November 1819 Hongi Hika sold to the Church of England Missionary Society 13,000 acres of land at Kerikeri, receiving forty-eight axes as payment. It was the first land transfer in New Zealand and was duly signed by both parties and their witnesses; both the vendor and the purchasers were satisfied with the deal.

This first purchase was like the first little wave that tops the bank of a stream in flood. Within the next twenty years such vast areas of Maori land had been allegedly bought by pakehas that the torrent threatened to sweep the banks away for ever.

As far as the Kerikeri sale was concerned, Hongi sold the lan d as a chief acting on behalf of his tribe, with the tribe's acquiescence and for the tribe's benefit. During the five years in which the missionaries had been under his protection, he had become well aware of what his people had gained through the presence of these pakehas; the sale of land would ensure their remaining at Kerikeri.

When the conditions of the times are taken into account, the price was a fair one. In fact the value of the axes to the tribe was probably greater than the value of the land, but that is something which would be almost impossible to assess, as all the usual factors taken into account nowadays in land valuation were then absent.

At the present time it is common enough for the seller of property to regret the sale a few years later if through some unforeseen reason land values have risen rapidly in that particular locality, but that does not make the original price unfair. Neither missionaries nor Maoris could have been expected to know what future developments were to take place in New Zealand; the formally attested sale at Kerikeri was a symbol of hope for stability in a land where all was in disorder.

But if that first sale was a fair one, the same could not be said of many of those which were to follow. By 1839, hundreds of land speculators had descended on the Maori, cajoling them with promises, plying them with grog, deceiving them with lies. Maoris equally astute sold land to which they had no shadow of right, or which they had no right to sell as individuals without the consent of the tribe. Often the same land was sold to several different pakehas; by the time the unsuspecting purchasers realised what had happened the Maori who had made the sales had disappeared and with him the goods which had been given in exchange.

A number of the chiefs, especially those of Northland, viewed the situation with alarm. Although many of them may have wished that they could go back to the ways of their ancestors, they were realistic enough to see that there could be no return to the past. But they realised that their own prestige was beginning to crumble and, with no authority to strengthen it or take its place, the future could only be chaos. Their apprehension was shared by many of the two thousand pakehas living in New Zealand at that time – traders menaced by insecurity, honest land purchasers who found their title challenged, missionaries angered by the exploitation of their Maori friends and converts.

The appointment of Busby as British Resident in 1833 without power to enforce his control was futile, but when Hobson became the first Governor seven years later, the British Government was prepared to take responsibility for his actions and gave him precise instructions as to his course. He was to take under British rule all areas of the North Island which the Maori people were willing to place under such sovereignty; the Maori people were to be treated justly and their welfare guarded; their land title was to be guaranteed and no land bought from them except by the Government.

No question of agreement with the Maoris of the south was mentioned. Hobson was to annex the South Island if he thought fit. Apparently the British Government believed that island to be almost uninhabited and Maori land claims non-existent.

It is clear that whatever injustices may have followed the establishment of British sovereignty in New Zealand, the intentions of the British Government towards the Maori people were fair and honourable.

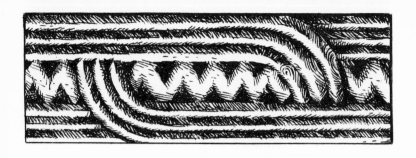

6
The Treaty of Waitangi

CAPTAIN HOBSON WASTED NO TIME in putting his instructions into effect, and presenting to the chiefs for discussion the terms of a treaty between Queen Victoria and the sovereign chiefs of New Zealand. The proposal was discussed in detail by the chiefs on the marae at Waitangi before a gathering of hundreds of their people, and the following day, 6 February 1840, eighty chiefs signed the treaty.

Prominent among the signatories was Tamati Waka Nene of the Ngapuhi tribe, a realist who saw that it was futile to bewail the past and who felt that the treaty could be a firm foundation on which to build a better future.

The terms of the treaty were:

1. The Chiefs assembled including Chiefs not present at the assembly hereby cede absolutely to the Queen of England for ever the Government of all their lands.

2. The Queen of England confirms and guarantees to the Chiefs and Tribes and to all the people of New Zealand the full possession of their lands, their homes and all their possessions, but the chiefs assembled and all other chiefs

yield to the Queen the right to alienate such lands which the owners desire to dispose of at a price agreed upon between the owners and person or persons appointed by the Queen to purchase on her behalf.

3. In consideration thereof, Her Majesty the Queen of England extends to the Natives of New Zealand Her Royal Protection, and imparts to them all the rights and privileges of British subjects.

These terms are given above in translation from the Maori version of the treaty. The English version was somewhat more precise, especially in Article 2, of which the first part reads:

Her Majesty, the Queen of England, confirms and guarantees to the Chiefs and Tribes of New Zealand, and to the respective families and individuals thereof, the full, exclusive and undisturbed possession of their Lands and Estates, Forests, Fisheries, and other properties which they may collectively or individually possess, so long as it is their wish and desire to retain the same in their possession.

Copies of the Treaty were carried to different parts of the country for discussion by the chiefs, and by the end of the year over five hundred Maoris had agreed to the provisions and signed the document.

It is significant that the chiefs who signed the Treaty were almost all from coastal areas; they had had much more contact with the pakeha, they were more aware of what European civilisation meant, in both its good and bad aspects, and they realised that the Treaty offered a possibility of protection by the Government against the demands of the flood of immigrants which they knew was coming.

In the preamble of the Treaty it was stated that the Queen desired the agreement with the chiefs 'by reason of the fact that so many members of her race were living in this land and many more were coming.' Many of the chiefs knew enough of world affairs to understand that the European powers were annexing and colonising land throughout the world, and they accepted the situation without considering

Signing the Treaty of Waitangi.

whether such actions were right or wrong. There was no clash with Maori custom in such annexations, and Te Rauparaha had just done exactly the same thing in the areas adjacent to Cook Strait. But, realising too that in far too many cases little regard had been paid to the rights of the original inhabitants, they were understandably perturbed at the prospect of large numbers of immigrants arriving in New Zealand. The Treaty offered them a chance that there would be orderly settlement in which their rights would be respected, whereas without it there could be no security whatsoever.

On the other hand the chiefs of the inland areas, in the heart of the Maori world into which only small numbers of pakehas had penetrated, took a very different view. Their own authority was still strong, they had less knowledge of the outside world and they felt confident that they would be able to resist whatever pressure might be exerted on them. Accordingly they were little disposed to give up even the shadow of their mana in return for protection which they felt they did not need.

Unfortunately, despite the good intentions of the Government, it was in difficulties immediately it began to put the Treaty into effect.

The New Zealand Company, organising the first planned colonisation of New Zealand, had purchased land for settlement from the Maoris in Taranaki, Wanganui, Wellington, and across Cook Strait in the South Island. Its agents regarded the Government's control of land sales as unwarranted interference and resented its investigation of their claims to land bought before the Treaty was signed. Many of the claims were challenged by the Maoris and found to be invalid when a Land Commissioner was appointed to investigate the matter.

The inquiries of the Commissioner were thorough and of necessity took many months. Meanwhile, settlers who had paid for their land before leaving England found themselves stranded, unable to take possession of their farms and not knowing whether their titles would be established or not. It was unfortunate but not surprising that in their frustration the prospective settlers, knowing nothing of Maori land custom, came to regard the Maori people as deliberately obstructive. As months and sometimes years went by the hostility of the settlers grew more bitter, not only towards the Maoris but also towards the Government officials and missionaries who understood and upheld Maori rights.

The situation could have been improved to some extent if the Government had been in a position to buy Maori land itself for the settlers. Some land which the owners were prepared to sell with a clear title was available, but the Government's finances were in no state to meet the demands on it.

Meanwhile the New Zealand Company tried to force the issue, with disastrous results. A survey of land at Wairau in Marlborough was resisted in 1843 by Te Rauparaha and his son-in-law Te Rangihaeata, who claimed rightly that it had not been sold, and urged that the matter be deferred until the Land Commissioner had held an enquiry. But the Company persisted, and a warrant for the arrest of Te Rauparaha was issued on a charge of having burnt a raupo hut that the surveyors had built.

An attempt at arresting the chief ended in complete failure. Instead, many of those who had accompanied the police officer were themselves captured by Te Rauparaha's men. But during the struggle random shots had been fired by both parties and one of those who had fallen dead was Te Rangihaeata's wife. In his grief the chief turned savagely on the prisoners and killed them to a man.

Captain Fitzroy, who had only just succeeded Hobson as Governor, was not willing to take drastic action against Te Rangihaeata in a case where the pakehas were so clearly in the wrong. But the shots fired at Wairau echoed throughout the whole country.

Neither Maori nor settler knew the whole story. To the pakeha, who felt that there could be no security in a country where such deeds went unpunished, it branded the Maori as a bloodthirsty savage; to the Maori it seemed that the pakeha was determined on aggression which could be resisted only by force.

The following year trouble flared up again, this time at the Bay of Islands – but for very different reasons.

The establishment of British rule had had unexpected effects among the Ngapuhi people. The sudden reduction of income caused by the ban on private land sales was taken in bad part by eager land-sellers who were not looking to the future but sought only immediate benefits. There were the delays during investigation of titles, and often a decision finally that the Government was unable to buy because of inadequate finances.

An attempt to build up those finances in what seemed the only possible way, by imposing customs dues, raised the price of goods bought by the Maoris, who found in addition that trade, their main source of steady income, had decreased seriously when the seat of government was transferred to a more central position at Auckland.

These problems were not insuperable, and the fact was realised by most of the Ngapuhi chiefs, but among them were some who took the limited view that British sovereignty was the sole cause of their troubles. A leader was found in Hone Heke, Hongi Hika's nephew, who expressed his feelings by the symbolical act of leading a small party to cut down the Government flagstaff at Russell. (Kororareka.)

There the matter might have ended if the growing tension among both Maori and pakeha had not made an inordinate obsession of the flagstaff. It was repeatedly re-erected and again cut down until the conflict developed into an attack on Russell itself on 10 March 1845 and finally became open war.

In October of that same year Governor Fitzroy was recalled and within a few weeks Captain George Grey took his place.

7
Governor Grey and Gathering Clouds

THE ONLY CHIEF OF NOTE who supported Hone Heke was Kawiti; others, in particular Tamati Waka Nene, condemned his actions and even took the field against him.

Nevertheless the rebels in their skilfully fortified pas were able to inflict defeats on British troops at Ohaeawai and Okaihau before the occupation of Kawiti's pa at Ruapekapeka on 11 January 1846 ended their resistance. The significance of the ill-advised conflict lay in the fact that Hone Heke had shown that pakeha troops were not invincible, that small numbers of determined Maoris in even hurriedly constructed defensive positions could resist regular soldiers with artillery support. Moreover the Maori ease of movement contrasted strongly with the slow advances made by the troops, hampered as they were with cannon and equipment.

The same year raiders from Te Rangihaeata's tribe attacked settlers in the Hutt valley. The Governor immediately ordered the arrest of Te Rauparaha whom he suspected with good reason of having instigated the raids, and the old warrior was not able to return from his internment in Auckland for eighteen months. Grey's action was undoubtedly illegal, but he felt that the situation was so dangerous that a decisive move was essential, and even the Ngatitoa people admitted that for once their chief had met his match.

A fortnight later Te Rangihaeata's pa was attacked; the chief withdrew inland under pressure from British troops and Maori warriors under the command of Wiremu Kingi Te Rangitake. Te Rangihaeata made no further move against the settlers.

Equally resolute action put an end to a flare-up at Wanganui in 1847. Here the Governor was accompanied by Tamati Waka Nene of Ngapuhi and Potatau Te Whero Whero of Waikato, both capable and influential chiefs.

It soon became clear to the settlers, too, that the Governor was a man to be reckoned with. In the last few months of his term of office, Governor Fitzroy had yielded to pressure and set aside the clause of the Treaty of Waitangi whereby Maori land could be sold only to the Government. Grey promptly reversed that decision, and made it clear that the Treaty would be adhered to strictly.

It must not be forgotten that the friction between colonists and Maoris was all taking place on the outer fringes of Maori territory. The inland tribes, secure in their roadless country still firmly under the control of their own chiefs, watched and waited to see what turn affairs would take.

But though there was cause for anxiety, the Maori people were making rapid material advances. The proportion of Maoris who could read and write was actually higher than that of the pakehas; most of the coastal shipping of the country was Maori owned and operated; not only those tribes whose land was close to pakeha settlements but also many of the people of more inland regions were becoming keen and capable farmers; most of the food consumed in New Zealand or exported in increasing quantities was produced on Maori farms, especially in the Waikato where good use was being made of the fertile soil.

The Governor did everything possible to help and encourage such activity, advancing loans where necessary to allow farm and other equipment to be bought. At the same time he realised that, for the good of the country as a whole, provision must also be made for the frustrated immigrants who were able and willing to work but unable to obtain the land they needed. Grey was an autocrat, but he was an autocrat who had the interest of both Maori and pakeha at heart, and it was obvious that a satisfactory solution of the land problem was the only possible foundation for goodwill between the two peoples.

The Governor was deeply impressed by the capability of the Maori people and although cynical observers commented that he made friends with them in order to persuade them to sell their land, there is no doubt that his close personal friendship with many of the leading chiefs such as Waka Nene, Te Whero Whero and Wiremu Kingi was genuine. A proficient speaker of the Maori language, Grey gained the confidence of the elders of the tribes. By publishing the mythology, legends and ancient songs which he learnt from their lips he ensured that the traditions of the people would never be lost.

Despite the fact that many Maori leaders were perturbed at seeing so much of the ancestral land of their people passing out of their hands, the voluntary sale of land went on, certainly more readily because of the personal respect in which the Governor was held. His method of overcoming the long delays which had been irritating to Maori and pakeha alike was to establish land titles at tribal meetings on the marae, and once they had been discussed and decided in that way there were few grounds for complaints that claims had been overlooked.

Nevertheless, however willingly certain tribes and their chiefs may have parted with their lands in return for money and goods, they could not help but observe uneasily that whereas they might be paid at the rate of a shilling an acre, that same land would be sold to pakeha settlers at ten shillings an acre or more! However they had confidence in the Governor who was clearly determined to uphold the Treaty of Waitangi and who was always prepared to listen to problems and redress grievances which they might bring to him. So long as Sir George Grey remained in office as a ruling governor, the Maori people felt that their rights would be respected.

The Maori was accustomed to personal rule; he felt uneasy when confronted with any form of control by a bureaucracy.

At the end of 1852 Grey left New Zealand on leave which ended with his appointment as Governor of Cape Colony. Almost his last official act, and one which was to cause grave misgivings among the Maoris, was the proclamation of the Constitution Act passed by the British Parliament. New Zealand was to have self-government, with Provincial Councils and a central Parliament, both elected by vote of the people.

It was an inevitable move; colonists who were used to ballot-box rule in Britain would not have been content to be governed indefinitely without parliamentary representation, and the franchise as granted in New Zealand was to be similar to that in England. But the all-important point to the Maori was that the vote in New Zealand, as in England, was dependant on property qualifications which, although fixed at a low level so that most pakehas were eligible, entirely excluded the Maori people from representation in the new Councils or Parliament. Maori individuals, as such, did not own land; the land belonged to the tribe.

The government was henceforth to be in the hands of the settlers; in view of past experience it is no wonder that the Maori people were apprehensive of what their doubtful future might hold.

The key point in the relationship between Maori and pakeha was Taranaki, and before long the eyes of both were turned on that province where a narrow strip of arable land lay hemmed in between the sea and the dense bush of the interior.

Waikato raids more than twenty years before had driven out the Atiawa people, all but a scattered remnant who were leading a precarious life in the devastated and weed-infested land of their ancestors. From these few needy Maoris, the New Zealand Company had bought land for settlement in Taranaki, probably in all good faith.

But the Waikato conquerors of Atiawa also had claims on Taranaki, and within a few years still more claimants arose. Slaves, carried off by the Waikato warriors and set free when their captors had become Christian, returned to their homes to find themselves dispossessed through a sale in which they had had no part. The final complication came in 1848 when Wiremu Kingi Te Rangitake led back many of his people from Waikanae where they had found refuge from the Waikato onslaught.

Wiremu Kingi was no enemy of the pakeha. An able man, educated in a mission school, he had done much to encourage his people to adopt what was useful in pakeha life and settle down in peaceful co-operation with the Wellington colonists. When the peace was disturbed by Te Rangihaeata, Wiremu Kingi had gone into action against him. He was certainly not the man to change character suddenly and become violently opposed to the Taranaki settlers without extreme provocation.

Unfortunately the provocation was there. The difficulty in establishing Maori rights of ownership had naturally led to very limited sales of land to colonists. In the whole province 63,000 acres had been sold, but there were about three thousand pakehas in the province clamouring for land, urging the Government to press for sales, and using every inducement to persuade the Maoris to agree.

The pakeha laboriously clearing a few acres of heavy bush looked resentfully at fertile land lying unused and covered in bracken at Waitara; but Waitara was Wiremu Kingi's ancestral home and his adamant refusal to sell is fully understandable.

However not all members of the Atiawa tribe were clear-sighted enough to see beyond the immediate advantages of selling the land, and against a confused background of claim and counter-claim, the animosity between Maoris who wished to sell and those who opposed further sales gathered intensity until it erupted into bitter conflict between tribes and sub-tribes. The Taranaki settlers, through lack of understanding of the real problem or sheer unscrupulous self-interest, all too frequently aided the minority of land-sellers with arms and ammunition.

In March 1859 came the crisis. Grey's successor as Governor, Colonel Gore Browne, despite his avowed intention of not interfering in Maori differences, could no longer ignore the disturbing situation in Taranaki. The Governor had prudently retained authority over Maori affairs instead of giving that control to the Provincial Councils or to Parliament, but because of his ignorance of the Maori language and unfamiliarity with Maori customs he was of necessity forced to rely on others as advisors. But his advisors were not always disinterested parties; in particular, the two men on whose advice he leaned when he went to Taranaki to address both Maori and pakeha on the land problem both had a close personal interest in the outcome of the affair.

Richmond, the Native Minister, was a Taranaki member of Parliament, dependent on the vote of the settlers whose demand for land had created the problem. McLean, the Land Purchase Commissioner, owed his status to his success in buying Maori land, but his prestige was suffering through his failure over the years to make any headway against Wiremu Kingi's determined objections.

Almost certainly without realising the full implications of his words, the Governor concluded a speech by announcing that he would buy no land without the owners' consent, but that he would not permit anyone to interfere in the sale of land unless he owned part of it. The crucial point was that the ariki did not own – as the pakeha interpreted it – any part of the tribal land as an individual, but by virtue of his rank he had an overriding control of it all.

To anyone familiar with Maori custom, there could be only one meaning in the Governor's words: henceforth offers to sell land made by individual rangatira would be accepted by the Government, and the ariki would have no power to intervene.

This disastrous pronouncement was to have repercussions far beyond the bounds of Taranaki, and must be considered against developments among the Maori people as a whole.

In the South Island with its sparse Maori population, there had been no serious difficulties after the Wairau affair in arranging land purchase terms satisfactory to both parties. The tribes near Wellington were in general prepared to sell land provided that sufficient remained for their own use. On the East Coast, Ngati-kahungunu and Ngati-porou saw only a few pakehas and no serious conflict of interests had developed; much the same situation was to be found along the eastern Bay of Plenty coast.

In their fastnesses of mountain and bush most of the Tuhoe tribe of the Urewera country had never seen a pakeha and went their own way little affected by events beyond their own land.

In the north, Tamati Waka Nene's influence was exercised to continue co-operation between Maori and pakeha; in any case the founding of Auckland had eased the pressure to sell land to settlers in Ngapuhi territories.

The Arawa tribes were in an unusual position. Many of the coastal people had migrated to work on the kauri-gum diggings in Northland; others again owned a fleet of coastal vessels with which they operated cargo services between Auckland and the many small ports scattered along the coasts between North Cape and Gisborne. There had been no large-scale attempt at settlement on their ancestral land and being successful through their own enterprise, the Arawa wished for no more than a continuation of the existing state of affairs.

Their kinsmen further south, the Tuwharetoa tribe, were too remote to be affected greatly by the presence of the pakeha, but they were influenced to some extent by their neighbours, Ngati-maniopoto.

It was the Waikato however, the heart of Maori territory, that by its position was destined to be the centre of the stage, and the Waikato chiefs were to take the lead among their people.

In this populous area, occupied by tribes loosely linked together by reason of their all being of Tainui descent, there was a considerable difference in development between the more remote Ngati-maniopoto in the southern sector and the tribes further north, where the farms and orchards produced large quantities of food for the Auckland market.

The three outstanding leaders among these tribes were Te Whero Whero, the old warrior leader of Ngati-mahuta, Wiremu Tamihana of Ngati-haua, son of Waharoa another famous warrior, and the fiery Rewi Manga of Ngati-maniopoto.

In 1854 a gathering of Taranaki and Wellington Maoris had met at Manawapou in south Taranaki to discuss problems which had arisen through the rapidly increasing settlement by the pakeha. It was no secret that immigration was building up pakeha numbers at an alarming rate; in fact within four years the Maori would be outnumbered. Clearly, the time had come for a unified policy, but although

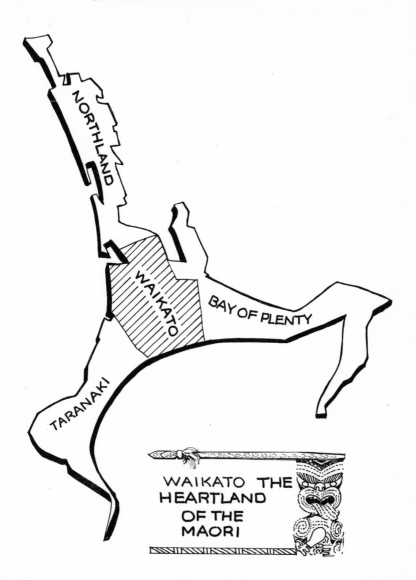

WAIKATO THE
HEARTLAND
OF THE
MAORI

the majority favoured a ban on land sales, no decision was made.

However the first step had been taken; from then on there would be increasing co-operation between tribes which in the past had often been bitter enemies.

Within a few years the move towards unity had developed into a definite plan, at least among the Tainui people. Tamihana Rauparaha of Ngati-toa, son of the old warrior chief, after a visit to England in 1851 was fired with the idea that just as the British people were united under the Queen so, too, a King of their own would bring unity to the Maori. His views were quickly taken up by others at assemblies of the tribes and discussed on the marae.

In 1858 the idea became a reality. Wiremu Tamihana of Ngati-haua, rebuffed and insulted by officials when he attempted to visit the Governor in Auckland the previous year, was told by an interpreter that if the Maoris wanted to improve their condition they should set about it themselves. The indignant chief took him at his word, and a few months later he had organised the election of a king.

Setting aside his own possible claim to the honour, he threw his considerable influence into support of Potatau Te Whero Whero of Ngati-mahuta, a chief whose mana stood high among the Tainui people. Potatau was duly elected, but died the following year to be succeeded by his son, Tawhiao.

Potatau was descended through a line of chiefs from Hoturoa, commander of the Tainui canoe and by his ancestry and reputation was well chosen to found a line of kings. Nevertheless, the driving force behind the King movement was Wiremu Tamihana, through whose descendants the title of Tumuaki (Head or President) has been inherited from father to eldest son.

The King movement had a different significance to different people. Primarily it was intended as a unifying factor with the King as a symbolical focal point for Maori loyalty.

It did not necessarily imply opposition to the pakeha, although events soon made it take that course; nor was it intended that the followers of the King should thereby forego their allegiance to the Queen.

The King was to be to the Maori people what the Governor was to the pakeha. The Government in New Zealand had become a purely pakeha government in which the Maori had no voice; he would therefore have his own parliament, elect his own representatives, and empower them under the sovereignty of the King to make laws for the Maori and ensure that they were obeyed.

The more extreme leaders such as Rewi had less real grasp of the situation. They visualised what the moderate leaders knew what was impracticable – complete independence and even the eventual expulsion of the pakeha. But however widely Maori opinions diverged, on one point the leaders were agreed: there must be no more sales of land.

It is against this broader background of the Maori world that the events in Taranaki must be regarded and Governor Gore Browne's ill-chosen words are seen not only as a thrust at the land policy of the great majority of the supporters of the King but also as an attack on the authority of the chiefs themselves.

Wiremu Kingi was no longer an individual chief defending his right to his ancestral home; the personal issue had become merged in a far greater question of principles in which all chiefs were vitally concerned.

8
Years of Disaster

WHEN GOVERNOR GORE BROWNE made his fateful announce-
ment that he intended to buy no land without the owner's
consent, but that he would allow no one to interfere unless
he owned part of it a sub-chief of Atiawa, Teira, immediately
offered a block of Waitara land for sale. Wiremu Kingi,
as ariki, flatly declared that the land was not to be sold and
left the meeting.

His action was a direct and open challenge to the
Governor's words and both Maori and pakeha tensely
awaited the outcome. They were not left long in doubt.
McLean, and Parris the local land purchase agent, who were
instructed by the Governor to investigate Teira's title to the
land, eventually stated that the title was clear. Wiremu
Kingi's protest was ignored, and in November 1859 part of
the purchase money was paid.

Three months later surveyors were ordered to begin
work at Waitara. Neither Maori nor pakeha had forgotten
that it was similar action which had led to the disastrous

affair of the Wairau sixteen years before; but whereas in the Wairau the issue had been forced by the New Zealand Company before a Government investigation had been made, in the Waitara case it was the Governor himself who was taking the decisive step. Moreover, he had made his intentions clear beforehand by sending troops to Taranaki and by declaring martial law in that province.

If there had been any hope in men's minds for a peaceful settlement it was dissipated entirely by the words in his proclamation that "active military operations" were "about to be undertaken by the Queen's forces against natives in the province of Taranaki in arms against her Majesty's authority."

Not warriors but old women met the surveyors, who were so persistently obstructed in their work that the survey could not proceed until troops had built and occupied a redoubt on the disputed land. Then at last Wiremu Kingi gave up all hope of averting the war which the pakeha was so clearly determined to force on him; the survey pegs were pulled up by Kingi's men who hastily constructed a pa not far away and prepared for the inevitable attack.

On 17 March 1860 pakeha guns opened fire on Kingi's pa and the Taranaki war had begun.

Before long Waikato warriors, against the wishes of Wiremu Tamihana, had come to Taranaki to take part in the struggle. Although Wiremu Kingi had at first refused allegiance to the Maori King, for tribal distrust had not entirely died away, he soon found that the former enemies of his tribe were now sharing a common cause with him. Soon he and his Atiawa declared their support of the King.

For over a year the conflict went on intermittently in Taranaki until finally in June 1861 an uneasy truce was called with the troops in possession of the Waitara region; but land south of New Plymouth at Tataraimaka, which had previously been bought by pakeha settlers, had passed into Maori hands.

By the terms of the agreement concluded between Gore Browne and Hapurona, who had been deputed by Wiremu Kingi to act on his behalf, the Waikato warriors were to leave Taranaki, the Atiawa people were to submit to the Queen's authority – which in fact they had never renounced – and return plunder taken from settlers' homes, the survey of the Waitara block was to be completed, and there was to be a further investigation into the whole question of its title. The important point for the Maori people was that the Governor had agreed to reopen the inquiry; everything depended on how thoroughly the investigation would be conducted, and whether the traditional rights of the ariki would be upheld or not.

There were some hopeful signs. Among the Maoris Wiremu Tamihana, a devout Christian, was still working hard for a peaceful solution of the problem, adhering to his watchword which had been adopted by the Maori King: Religion, Love, and Law.

Many pakehas too, were outspoken in their condemnation of the aggressive policy of the settlers. Sir William Martin, the Chief Justice, his friend Bishop Selwyn, Archdeacon Octavius Hadfield, and William Fox, leader of the Opposition in Parliament, all urged the Governor to use restraint and ensure that justice was done. But by this time the Governor's pride had been touched; he felt that he could not tolerate the challenge to his authority which he considered inherent in the existence of a Maori King, and began to prepare plans to overthrow the King by force.

Gore Browne was destined never to carry out those plans. In October 1861 he was superseded, and Sir George Grey returned to New Zealand in his place. Three months earlier the Government had lost office and Fox had become Prime Minister.

It now remained to be seen whether the tension which was building up in New Zealand could be relieved or whether it had gone beyond control.

Grey's return late in 1861, was received by the Maori people with mixed feelings. They remembered that he had been their friend in the past but many of the old chiefs who had known him so well had since died and a new generation was beginning to take control, a generation embittered by years of friction with the pakeha and resentful of the injustice of Governor Gore Browne's actions in Taranaki. The previous governor had shown open hostility to the King movement; there were still six thousand British troops in New Zealand and Grey's reputation as a man of action had not been forgotten. Was Gore Browne recalled simply to ensure that the Maori should be crushed efficiently by a more capable man?

In that atmosphere of uncertainty and suspicion it is not surprising that Grey reported that he found the chiefs "exasperated, sullen and desperate."

Wiremu Tamihana's mana among the followers of the King, although still strong was no longer what it had been; Rewi Manga Maniopoto was growing more and more vehement in his appeals to drive out the pakeha, and when emotions were stirred by fiery speeches even the most moderate of the Waikato people began to doubt if peace was possible.

Even if Grey had wished to reduce the numbers of troops, it is doubtful if the New Zealand Government would have permitted it, for the settlers of Auckland and Taranaki did not regard Rewi's threats as idle words. Although Grey honestly desired peace, he would have been failing in his duty if he had not taken precautions against a possible attack; accordingly he began a project which in that electrified atmosphere only served to confirm Maori opinion that he really intended war. He pushed ahead with an extension of the road from Drury into the lower Waikato.

Meanwhile Grey was also planning a system of government for the Maori territories by indirect control. The scheme envisaged the sub-division of all Maori land into

twenty areas, each of which would have a pakeha commissioner, but all the remaining police and magistrates were
to be Maori. Law-making was to be in the hands of a council
of magistrates presided over by the commissioner.

As far back as 1846 the British Government had made
provision for the establishment of such districts in which the
Maori people were to live under laws of their own making,
but nothing had been done to implement the scheme. In
1861 it was too late; the Maori had done for himself what the
pakeha had promised but failed to carry out. He was by this
time not prepared to accept the new proposals as anything
but an attempt to overthrow the King and strengthen
pakeha grip on his land.

The views of the Maori leaders were well known to their
people but not only through words spoken in assemblies.
Realising the power of the press, King Tawhiao had authorised the establishment of a Maori newspaper with the
ominous name "Te Hokioi" – the bird which screams in the
night as a warning of pestilence or war. The editor chosen
was King Potatau's cousin, Patara, a man whose keenly
logical and often witty arguments carried great weight.

So considerable was the influence of "Te Hokioi" that
Grey ordered John Gorst, a magistrate stationed at Te
Awamutu to set up a rival paper. "Te Pihoi Mokemoke i
runga i te Tuanui". Accordingly the two newspapers fought
a verbal battle for several months until Rewi, stung by Gorst's
words attacking the king, suppressed his paper and ordered
him to leave the district within three weeks.

But Taranaki still smouldered on, with pakehas holding
Waitara and Maoris occupying Tataraimaka, which they
declared would not be relinquished until Waitara was handed
back.

By 1863 the Governor had become convinced that the
seizure of Waitara had been illegal; he informed the Government of his views and on 11 May the area was given up. But
this act of justice which might have done much to ease the

tension if it had occurred a few weeks earlier was rendered utterly useless through an extraordinary error of judgment.

On 4 April British troops had occupied Tataraimaka – while Grey's intentions towards Waitara were still unknown. All Rewi's warnings against pakeha treachery appeared to be justified, and when the Ngati-maniopoto chief sent out a message to kill the pakehas the Taranaki people were moved to take reprisals. A party of soldiers was ambushed and of ten men only one escaped – on 4 May seven days before the Waitara block was formally restored to Maori ownership.

Whether it would have been possible to avert war at this late stage is doubtful; extremists on both sides were in the ascendancy. Rewi's voice was heard above Wiremu Tamihana's, and Grey the autocrat, grown more irascible with the years, was determined to impose his authority on the Maoris over whom the power of his personality had waned.

On 12 July 1863 General Cameron's soldiers crossed the Mangatawhiri stream and the invasion of the Waikato began under the orders of the Governor. The reasons given by Grey were that Waikato chiefs had instigated or approved the Taranaki ambush, had sheltered men who had committed crimes elsewhere, had driven peaceful pakehas out of the Waikato and had threatened to attack the Auckland settlers. He claimed that it was essential to establish law and order by setting up military posts throughout the area.

Tamihana's worst fears were realised. There was now no option for him but to abandon his efforts for peace (since events were beyond his control) and unite the Waikato tribes in defence of their ancestral homes.

Despite their courage the warriors of the Waikato tribes could not resist indefinitely the greater numbers and superior weapons of the troops. The determined defence of Rangiriri, the battle at Orakau where the indomitable Rewi hurled his defiant words at the encircling attackers, *"Ka whawhai tonu. Ake! Ake! Ake!", will never be forgotten, but ultimate

*"We shall fight on. Forever! Forever! Forever!"

defeat was inevitable. By July 1864 the Waikato was lost, the Ngaiterangi tribe of Tauranga, after a victory at Gate Pa, had been overwhelmed at Te Ranga, and further effective resistance was no longer possible.

The chivalrous courage of the Maoris had won the admiration and respect of their military opponents, who sympathised with the defeated tribesmen and made no secret of their own disgust at taking part in an unjust war; but sympathy was little recompense for the Waikato exiles who from beyond the Puniu stream at Te Awamutu and on the rugged slopes of Maungatautari mountain saw their fertile lands in the grip of their conquerors.

In 1863 the New Zealand Government had passed the New Zealand Native Land Settlements Act which made its intentions perfectly clear. Over two million acres of Maori land were to be confiscated, slightly more than half being in the Waikato and the rest in Taranaki.

Despite the claim that the war was being fought to establish law and order among lawless tribes, it was significant to all that Ngati-maniopoto, who had been the most ready to resort to violence, lost no land whatever, whereas the other Waikato tribes which had shown far more tolerance and willingness to co-operate with the pakeha were to be deprived of a vast area of their most fertile land.

To both pakeha and Maori it was obvious that whatever reasons might have been put forward to justify the invasion, its only real purpose was the acquisition of land.

On 17 May 1865 Wiremu Tamihana, speaking for the majority of the Waikatos, accepted the facts of the disastrous situation and acknowledged defeat. Beyond the confiscation line, King Tawhiao remained aloof among Ngati-maniopoto with those of the Waikato people who refused to submit – but the Waikato war was over.

9
The Darkness and the Gleams

MILITARY DEFEAT, THE SPREAD OF DISEASE as conditions became more and more unsettled, and the loss of their land, plunged some of the tribes into the depths of despair. It seemed to them that they were a doomed race which would soon disappear before the inexorable pressure of the pakeha.

Even the Christian religion which they had adopted sincerely, began to appear to be a shrewd device of the pakeha to weaken their will to fight or retain their lands. Bishop Selwyn, that sincere friend of the Maori, was seen among troops before a battle; many Maoris came to believe that, as their tohungas of former days had done, he was there to urge the troops on to destroy them.

The emotional stress that they were suffering under affected different people in different ways. Some tried to accept the bitter situation and adapt themselves to the changed conditions, some lapsed into sullen apathy, others again became filled with a fanatical hatred of the pakeha and all his ways. It was these last who turned away angrily from

Christianity which appeared to have failed them in their need and followed prophets who preached new religions and a holy war, promising ultimate victory for those who believed.

The first prophet to arise was Te Ua Haumene of Wai-totara, founder of the Pai Marire religion. Claiming to have been instructed in visions by the Angel Gabriel, Te Ua promised all true believers immunity from bullets and ordered that the head of a pakeha captain killed in a skirmish with Te Ua's followers should be preserved in the ancient manner and carried round the country as an oracle.

The tohungas, whose mana had been steadily passing away, were among the first to give support, realising that this new religion could give them opportunities to exert again their ancient influence over the people.

Soon rituals were developed in which Pai Marire devotees marched around niu flagpoles chanting an incomprehensible blend of Christian and Old Testament phrases with military commands, interspersed with a barking "Hau", from which the sect came to be known as Hauhaus.

From Taranaki bands of Hauhaus went in 1865 through the country to the East Coast, preaching their doctrines and stirring up an almost hypnotic excitement in the tribes. The leaders of the King movement at first welcomed this new source of strength for their dispirited men, probably not from religious conviction, but from political motives, to strengthen Maori nationalism. The Hauhau emissaries were well received making many converts as they went, even among such tribes as Ngatikahungunu who had taken no part in the Taranaki or Waikato wars.

But some tribes stood out firmly in opposition to the fanatical doctrines. The Arawa people, whose lands had not been threatened by the pakeha and who had adopted a policy of co-operation and commercial enterprise, had not joined the King movement. They remained neutral during the wars until King supporters from the eastern Bay of

Plenty tribes tried to cross Arawa territory on their way to the Waikato. From then on the Arawas were allies of the pakeha troops, and strong contingents from the tribe took part in subsequent actions.

The majority of Ngati-porou under Ropata Wahawaha, and the Wanganui people led by Kepa Te Rangihiwinui were strongly opposed to the Hauhaus and were in action against them, both independently and in alliance with the troops.

In fact, although the Hauhaus for various reasons gained supporters rapidly in the initial stages of their defiance of the pakeha, they quickly alienated the sympathy of chiefs who were disgusted at their excesses, in particular the barbarous murder of Mr Volkner, a missionary at Opotiki. Soon Maori contingents, even including some who had supported the King in the Waikato war, were joining the pakeha to hunt down the Hauhaus who had brought shame on their people.

A campaign on the East Coast in 1866 ended with the defeat of the Hauhaus and the deportation of a considerable number of prisoners to the Chatham Islands; but among them was a man whose name was later to become the terror of Maori and pakeha, Te Kooti Rikirangi. Although he had fought against the Hauhaus, he was banished without trial on what seems to have been a trumped-up charge.

During his exile his mana steadily increased among the prisoners until eventually he led them in seizing a vessel and returning to New Zealand in 1868. With nearly three hundred followers – men, women and children – he landed at Poverty Bay, declaring that he had no wish to fight and desired only to lead his people in peace to the King Country. However despite the recommendations of pakehas who had a better understanding of the Maori people than the Government had, it was decided to hunt him down.

Immediately Te Kooti began to strike back with the skill of an extremely able guerilla leader. Nursing his bitter grievance, he made his attacks on both pakeha and Maori swiftly and ruthlessly, sparing neither women nor children.

At the same time, in Taranaki, Titokowaru fanned the flickering embers of Hauhauism into flame again, but his revival of long-abandoned cannibalism in order to terrorise his opponents, roused the anger and repugnance of the great majority of the Maori people and a large force of Maoris and troops gave him no rest until he finally fled to sanctuary in the upper reaches of the Waitara River in 1869.

Te Kooti was a much more formidable opponent but after four years of sudden raids and long persistent hunts he was finally penned in the dense bush of the Urewera country. In May 1872, he eluded his pursuers to escape to the King Country, where he was left unmolested. As with Titoko-waru, it was felt that the chance of his becoming a menace again was remote.

Despite his reputation for ferocity, there was another side to Te Kooti's character which has had a more lasting effect. Together with many of the generation which had grown up during the years of bitterness and conflict, he no longer looked on the Christian faith as the first converts had done. It was a pakeha religion, too closely identified with every-thing that was alien to the ancient culture of the Maori. In their search for a faith which could help them to rise above despair and inspire Maori nationalism to continue its re-sistance, the Hauhaus had turned to a wild parody of religion, to a blood-cult that sanctioned even cannibalism. But Te Kooti was no mentally unbalanced Te Ua. His mind was quick and alert, and pondering over religion during his months of exile he was brought at last to a new expression of the Christian faith – not a blind acceptance of pakeha Christianity, but a genuine Maori interpretation of it. Ringatu, the new religion to which he converted his wild Hauhau followers, was no reversion to heathen barbarism. Its prayers, hymns, psalms and scriptural passages were all Christian; so too was its Communion Service, but so repugnant was cannibalism to Te Kooti that he would not allow the symbolic bread and wine of that service to have a counterpart in Ringatu.

In the days of tribulation of the Maori people, he felt himself to be a prophet leading his followers out of bondage; and many Old Testament prophets were no less truculent towards their enemies than was Te Kooti.

The fear that he inspired has died away, but his teachings still live. Today five thousand people of the Ureweras and regions nearby are adherents of the faith that Te Kooti preached, worshipping the God of the Christian Bible, but in a Maori way.

The major cause of the wars in Taranaki and the Waikato was the demand for land, so that it is not surprising that steps should have been taken by the Government to make land sales easier. Nevertheless, the setting up of the Native Land Court in 1865 was a genuine attempt to give fair treatment to the Maori people and to eliminate the causes of friction in the past.

The Government abandoned its absolute monopoly over Maori land purchases and allowed land which had been through the Court to be bought by private individuals also. No land was to be sold without a clear title but once the Court had thoroughly investigated claims and established ownership, an area of land was held under a title recognised by pakeha law.

Any land could be the subject of investigation by the Court if the owners wished, regardless of whether they intended to sell it or not, but in practice the majority of cases were brought by intending land-sellers. The freehold title to a block of land could be granted to multiple owners, or if owners desired they could receive individual titles to the fractions of a partitioned block.

The dealings of the Land Court were painstakingly just, but the establishment of personal land titles automatically extinguished tribal rights and effectively nullified the right of veto of the ariki who found himself one among many owners of the tribal lands. Henceforth, whatever authority he might possess would depend on his personal mana, not on customary or legal rights.

It is easy to be wise after the event, but it can now be seen that the weakness in the system established for the sale of land lay in the fact that there was no effective impartial advisor for the inexperienced Maori who suddenly found himself possessing marketable property.

Individual thrift, the banking of savings, and investment for the future played no part in the communal life of the kainga. The land-seller suddenly found himself wealthy, envied by his friends, and able to gratify every whim – while the purchase money lasted. He was able to buy what seemed to him unlimited quantities of liquor, and for many its fatal attraction was irresistible. It is significant that in 1884 the Government, acting on King Tawhiao's personal petition, banned licensed hotels from the King Country.

Before 1860 about seven million acres of land had been sold, but the Maori still retained about 21 million acres. During the Waikato war, three million acres were confiscated by proclamation although in actual fact half of that land was not taken and the original owners returned to it.

By 1891 only 11 million acres remained, including much that was useless for settlement. It is noteworthy that by that year there were some who realised that land not required for immediate use could bring in profits in another way; two and one-half million acres of Maori land were being farmed by pakehas under leasehold.

To many pakehas it seemed that the Maoris were a dispossessed people heading for extinction, gazing apathetically into a hopeless future, or seeking by wild extravagance and drunkenness to forget the fate that awaited them.

Such a gloomy picture is a sweeping generalisation and far from the truth, but one fact could not be disputed. Even though the methods of assessment may have been faulty, successive censuses revealed that the number of Maoris was decreasing. In the census of 1858, 56,000 Maoris had been recorded; this number had steadily dropped until in 1896 there were 42,000. Apart from the possibility of errors in enumeration, one factor could have had a slight influence on the totals; half-castes living as pakehas were counted as Europeans, and undoubtedly more were living as pakehas in 1896 than was the case forty years previously.

However that would not account for a difference of 14,000, and the figures were certainly alarming for the leaders of the Maori people.

There is no need to conjure up some mysterious psychological fatalism which was driving the people to extinction. The decrease can be adequately explained by the ravages of pakeha diseases among men, women and children living in fearfully insanitary surroundings. However much they were advised to improve conditions, there was a deep-rooted suspicion of pakeha advice, especially so when, even with the best of intentions, the pakeha urged them to abandon the ways of their ancestors.

Pakeha medical knowledge had made tremendous advances since the Treaty of Waitangi but many of the Maori people were at least forty years behind. Tuberculosis, pneumonia and typhoid, which in the middle of the century carried off thousands in the crowded and insanitary cities of England, were in 1890 still ravaging the Maoris who had not yet learnt how to guard against them.

Although pakehas of goodwill might do their best to help, their efforts were insufficient alone to break down the barriers of distrust or frightened bewilderment. Only through men of their own people, trained in the medical knowledge of the pakeha yet understanding the Maori mind, was salvation to come.

The key to a brighter future for the Maori people was education. From the days of the early missionaries this fact had been recognised; a school became an essential feature of every mission settlement. Under an Ordinance passed in 1847 mission schools were to receive Government subsidies, and by 1852 there were 700 pupils in such schools. But more than the rudiments of education were needed if Maori clergy were to be ordained and in founding St John's College Bishop Selwyn envisaged a school in which Maori and pakeha were to be trained together, leading on to a college for higher education.

Even though St John's College ran into difficulties and for a time was closed, a start had been made; and the work was continued later with St Stephen's College.

In 1853, Sir George Grey gave 4,000 acres of land at Te Aute in Hawke's Bay for a Maori boarding school, and the local Maori people gave an equal amount. Archdeacon Samuel Williams undertook the task of converting a wilderness of fern and bush into a productive farm which would not only support the proposed school but also give scope for practical training to the boarders. So began Te Aute College, which was to play such an outstanding part in producing leaders of the Maori people two generations later.

By the Native Schools Acts of 1867 and 1871, the Government took over the responsibility for providing education for Maori children, although still continuing to subsidise existing mission schools, and soon Government Maori schools began to appear scattered through the areas with a predominantly Maori population. As it was realised that a Maori knowing little English would be seriously handicapped in the future, one of the clauses in the Acts laid down that all instruction should be given in the English language.

By 1884, over 2,000 pupils were being educated in purely Maori schools, including both State and mission schools; perhaps almost as many other Maori children were attending public schools in areas where Maoris did not predominate.

But of these only a handful were going on to higher

education in secondary schools and as yet none whatever had reached the University stage. What no one realised was that among the children still in those primary schools were the future outstanding leaders of the Maori people, men whose ability and persistence were to break through resentment, despondency and ancient conservatism and set the feet of the Maori on a new road of hope.

The new dawn was coming, but one generation earlier there was a forerunner to the dawn, one whose name was to be held in high esteem among both Maori and pakeha – Timi Kara, Sir James Carroll.

Son of Tapuke, a high chieftainess of Ngatikahungunu, and her pakeha husband, Joseph Carroll, the first settler in Wairoa, Timi Kara was given a full education in the traditional learning of the Maori. In pakeha knowledge his formal schooling ended at 10, but with the active encouragement and help of his parents and Maori relatives Timi Kara's alert mind never ceased learning.

Nor was his body less vigorous than his mind. At the age of seventeen he demonstrated his courage and endurance by taking part in five strenuous months of campaigning against Te Kooti in the Ureweras, before beginning what was to be his life work.

After a short period in the office of the Commissioner of Native Affairs at Napier his ability was recognised; he was transferred to the Native Department in Wellington and at the age of twenty-one was appointed interpreter of the House of Representatives, a position for which his fluency in both the Maori and English languages fitted him admirably.

He missed no opportunities for acquiring knowledge. In his first years in the Native Commissioner's office he was encouraged to read good English books and it is said that his outstanding command of that language came from his intensive study of them, especially the Bible and Shakespeare's works. Four years later he sought the wider field of politics, and eventually in 1887 was elected as the member for Eastern Maori.

Maori representation in Parliament dated from 1868, and although boundaries have altered somewhat, there have always been the same four electorates. However until Timi Kara entered Parliament the Maori members had tended to restrict their speeches mainly to Maori affairs. Several of them were capable speakers who expressed the Maori point of view clearly to the House, but all were diffident in discussing what they felt to be purely pakeha matters.

But Timi Kara had been trained in both cultures, he understood both the pakeha and the Maori mind, and he spoke as a New Zealander. It says much for his prestige that after representing Eastern Maori in two successive parliaments he stood for a pakeha electorate, Waiapu, in 1893 and was again elected; for the next twenty-six years he remained the member for Waiapu, later renamed Gisborne.

During almost the whole of his long term in Parliament he was a member of Cabinet, either as representative of the Maori people or as the actual Minister for Native Affairs, and in recognition of his work he was created K.C.M.G. in 1911.

Despite the well-earned honours that came his way and his prestige among the pakeha as Sir James Carroll, he was still Timi Kara to the Maori and never ceased to strive tolerantly and good-humouredly for mutual understanding and friendship between the two peoples.

Long before his death in 1926 Timi Kara was able to see his ideals taken up enthusiastically and capably by the next generation. He had surveyed the route and cut the first track through the tangle that lay ahead of the Maori; it was for those who followed to widen the track to a broad highway along which in future time their people could march confidently ahead.

Although he himself had received no secondary schooling, Timi Kara fully realised that only through education could the Maori hope to take his rightful place in the days that lay ahead. It was to the secondary schools and to Te Aute in particular that he looked for the new dawn – and he was not disappointed.

10
The New Dawn

WHEN ANY HUMAN SOCIETY begins to break down, whether the collapse is due to external pressure or internal decay, its regeneration can be successful only if it produces its own leaders, enlightened men who can win the confidence of their own people and lead them along the way of survival. But many ways which appear to offer hope may prove to be only blind alleys in which the lost people grope despairingly.

The ultimate leaders must be men of courage, not easily disheartened when their people fail to respond – but they need more than courage alone. They must have the clear vision to see the road ahead, the broader view which so often can come only by withdrawing from among their people for a while either physically or mentally. Such a withdrawal gives the scene its true proportions and perspective; the foreground which had loomed so large that it blotted out everything beyond it can be seen for what it really is, and the leader returns enlightened to draw his people on.

So it has been with the Maori people. The boys who left their villages for boarding schools were not lost to their own kin. Rather they were the leaders who gained enlightenment by their withdrawal. They went as young Ngatiporou, Te Atiawa, Ngati-kahungunu, boys of all the many tribes which were represented at Te Aute; they returned as young Maoris with a new consciousness of Maoritanga, a broader view of the problems of the whole Maori people, and a determination to urge others to follow the road ahead.

The senior boys of Te Aute were becoming increasingly aware of the havoc that disease was creating among their people and the extent to which their mode of life was responsible for the tragic situation. It was not easy to convince their more conservative elders, but in the college there was growing a spirit of single-minded devotion that was not to be turned aside.

Te Aute had been singularly fortunate in its headmasters. Archdeacon Samuel Williams, that trusted friend of the Maori people, had guided its development during its early years. Then in 1878 John Thornton took up the task which he did not relinquish until thirty-four years later. His mind was attuned to those of the pupils in his care, his theme was that they should strive continually, not for selfish ends but for the good of their people, and his devoted personality won loyalty in its turn. The boys of Te Aute courageously took up the challenge.

Rewiti Kohere has related how he and two other boys, Timutimu Tawhai and Maui Pomare, spent a month's holiday in the winter of 1889 on a walking tour, visiting as many kainga as possible in Hawke's Bay to expound the central theme of their doctrine: the world was not as it had been in the days of their ancestors. Times were changing, and the Maori way of life must move with the times if the Maori people were to survive.

Two years later a number of older boys at the college followed up this pioneering effort by founding an organisation with similar views, "The Association for the Amelioration of the Conditions of the Maori Race." The task that had been undertaken was no easy one and there were discouraging set-backs in the early stages, but from that first organised group grew the "Te Aute College Students' Association" which later, in order to admit old boys from other Maori schools, changed its name to "The Young Maori Party". The renaissance of the Maori people had begun.

Among the many able Maori leaders in that renaissance, three were outstanding: Apirana Turupa Ngata, Maui Pomare and Te Rangihiroa (Peter Henry Buck).

Apirana Ngata, son of Paratene Ngata, chief of Ngati-porou, was born at Kawakawa Bay near East Cape in 1874. After qualifying at Te Aute College for entrance to University in 1890, he went to Canterbury College where he made history by gaining his B.A. three years later, the first Maori to graduate. In 1894 he advanced to M.A. at Auckland University College, with Honours in Political Science and the following year completed the requirements for LL.B.

After being admitted as a barrister and solicitor in 1896 he followed his profession as a lawyer in Auckland until, three years later, he was appointed travelling secretary of the Te Aute College Students' Association. Ngata's life-work of service, not solely for his own people but for all New Zealanders, had fairly begun.

Meanwhile Pomare, one of the three boys in the pioneer journey of 1889, had also been pursuing higher studies in preparation for a life devoted to helping others. Maui Pomare was a son of Naera Pomare, chief of Ngati-mutunga, a sub-tribe of Te Atiawa, which had accompanied Te Rauparaha from Taranaki to Kapiti; and on his mother's side he was connected with the Ngati-toa tribe and Te Rauparaha himself.

Maui Pomare was born in 1876 near Urenui in Taranaki and attended various Maori primary schools. But in 1887 he was enrolled at Christchurch Boys' High School, following the last wishes of his father, who had recently died, that he should seek the wisdom of the pakeha and bring it back to his own people. For two years he boarded in Christchurch during the school terms, spending the holidays in the Chatham Islands with his mother who was living there on land conquered by Ngati-mutunga fifty years previously.

Then came the death of his mother and he passed into the care of an aunt in Auckland who transferred him to Te Aute College. In 1893 came the decisive move on which his whole future career was to depend: he left for the United States to study medicine at Battle Creek Seventh Day Adventist Missionary College in Michigan. It says much for his courage and tenacity of purpose that among strangers and so far from home he persevered doggedly with his studies, paying his way through university by vacation work of whatever kind was available and by lecturing in public on Maori life and traditions.

After preliminary training at Battle Creek Pomare went on to the American Medical Missionary College at Chicago where in 1899 he graduated M.D.

In the same year, Te Rangihiroa, another Ngati-mutunga old boy of Te Aute, began his studies at Otago University accompanied by Tutere Wirepa of Ngati-porou. Both successfully completed their courses by gaining degrees in medicine.

Te Rangihiroa was born only a few miles away from the birthplace of Maui Pomare. There is some uncertainty about the date, but 1877 appears most probably correct. His father was William Henry Buck, whose wife, the chieftainess Ngarongo-ki-tua, adopted him when his mother Rina, her cousin, died shortly after he was born.

No sooner had he graduated M.D. at Otago than he became associated with Pomare in the crusade for health that would eventually bring the Maori people out of the valley of the shadow and set their feet firmly on the pathway of hope.

The new dawn was breaking.

By 1894 the old order in the Maori world was passing away. Almost all the great Maori leaders of the years of conflict were gone. Wiremu Tamihana had died less than two years after the end of the war in the Waikato; within the twelve years from 1882, Wiremu Kingi, Titokowaru, Te Kooti, Rewi Manga Maniopoto, Te Heuheu Tukino Horonuku of Ngati-Tuwharetoa, and King Tawhiao had all passed on, and Ropata Wahawaha, their former foe, was soon to follow them at the great age of ninety.

Only one great leader of the earlier generation remained: a man of peace, Te Whiti Orongomai, a chief of Te Atiawa in Taranaki. Te Whiti had taken no part in the wars, either in support of Wiremu Kingi or of Titokowaru, although he had given shelter after hostilities ended to Wiremu Kingi. Instead he had remained quietly at Parihaka, urging his people to remain aloof from the pakeha and renounce violence.

He felt, as so many others did, that pakeha Christianity had failed the Maori, but for Te Whiti there must be no return to the barbaric gods of ancient times. The doctrines which he preached were a Maori adaptation of Christianity in which he sought, as did Te Kooti, to retain what he felt to be the best of pakeha teachings. Honesty, justice, industry, cleanliness and abstention from alcohol were the basic tenets of his creed.

But Te Whiti was fully conscious of the injustice which had deprived his people of their land. The claims to their lost territories must never be abandoned until the pakeha made amends for the wrong he had committed. Yet violence must be met, not with violence but with the moral force of passive resistance. The time was to come when Te Whiti's aims would be achieved, but not until many years after he himself had passed away.

Eventually in 1881, after Te Whiti's followers had attempted to assert their rights to the confiscated land by symbolically ploughing furrows across farms occupied by pakeha settlers and by removing survey pegs, the Government decided to take action. An armed force was sent to Parihaka, the settlement was destroyed and many of the leaders, including Te Whiti, were arrested and deported.

But the prophet's people held firmly to his principles of non-violence; there was no resistance to the arrests, and the Parihaka people stood by passively as their homes went up in flames.

Although the Government had achieved its aim by force, the moral victory lay with Te Whiti, and when after two years the deportees were allowed to return, the prophet's followers increased rapidly in numbers throughout the whole country. For the next twenty years the adherents to his creed held themselves apart in proud isolation, asserting their resistance to the injustices of the past by complete refusal to co-operate in all that was associated with the pakeha. Pakeha schools and pakeha medicine alike were forbidden to the followers of Te Whiti.

Maui Pomare knew the prophet well; he was of the same tribe and in his childhood he had lived at Parihaka until its destruction in 1881. He respected Te Whiti as a man, but he realised too that so long as the old chief lived there was little hope of convincing his people that the way which they had chosen was one without a future.

In 1900, just before the return of Pomare from the United States with high qualifications in medicine, the Public Health and Maori Councils Act was passed by the Government in which, it must be remembered, Timi Kara was a member of the Cabinet.

Under the new Act, New Zealand was to be divided into nineteen districts, each of which was to be governed by an elected Council with powers similar to those of a Borough Council. A Native Health Officer was to be appointed with authority to investigate health, sanitation and water supplies in Maori villages, and to instruct the people in the principles of health, hygiene and general welfare.

Maui Pomare was the obvious choice for the position of Health Officer, and within a very short time he had begun his work. No one knew better than he the magnitude of the task which would have appalled a lesser man. He well realised that drastic action – an overturning of traditional habits and cherished beliefs, a complete change in the Maori way of life – was the only way in which his people could be saved.

No pakeha could have achieved that aim. Even for Pomare, young and vigorous, well-educated, capable, and a chief by birth, there were times when he felt that he was attempting the impossible, that he could perhaps postpone but not prevent the extinction of his people.

The older generation of tohungas had passed away. They had at least been honest in their attempts to cure, and saw with gloomy bewilderment that to cope with the diseases of the pakeha was beyond their power. But now a new generation arose – self-appointed tohungas, shrewd men who realised how the situation could be turned to their own financial advantage. The dispirited people, suspicious of everything pakeha, clung desperately to whatever remained of the life of their ancestors, and the tohungas widened the breach between the two races. If their treatment succeeded, they took the credit to themselves; but if it failed, the pakeha was blamed for the disease.

Pomare quickly realised that the hard core of resistance to his work lay in the tohungas. The Maori was doomed unless the power of those charlatans could be broken, and he set out with determination to loosen their grip. But officialdom was hard to convince and pakeha public opinion was apathetic.

It was not until 1907 that the Tohunga Suppression Act was passed and the Health Officer had the support of the law to help him in the struggle. There were many years of hard work still ahead, but with the outlawing of the tohunga the force of positive opposition steadily waned.

Among his own tribe, Pomare was content to wait until the personal influence of Te Whiti ended but among others he threw himself vigorously into the battle for health. Despite horrified objections from tribal elders he destroyed with fire hundreds of derelict dwellings, haunts of rats and disease, which the observance of tapu had left untouched in the midst of populous villages.

Yet although he attacked with determination the ancient practices which were destroying his people, Pomare never failed to observe the niceties of traditional etiquette. His method was always to persuade, to convince the villagers on the marae, to speak to them as a Maori to Maoris – and only as a last resort, when every other method had failed and the situation was desperate, would he invoke the law to enforce his reforms.

In November 1907 Te Whiti died, leaving his own people and his followers throughout New Zealand without a leader. Tactfully but skilfully Maui Pomare seized the opportunity which then presented itself; he paid an honest tribute to the memory of a sincere man whose only thought was for his people but pointed out that change was now inevitable. Te Whiti's followers must look henceforth to the future – the past was gone beyond recall.

With Pomare's guidance the Maori Union, a purely Taranaki organisation, was formed to give leadership and advice in bettering the conditions of life and under two chiefs, Te Kahupukoro and Tahupotiki Haddow, the latter an ordained minister in the Methodist Church, it steadily gained in strength.

In 1905 Pomare gained his able assistant, Te Rangihiroa, who had just completed his medical degree at Otago

University and as the arduous years passed by the results of their work began to show. Health Inspectors were appointed to assist the Health Officer in his task; some were Maori, others pakehas deeply interested in Maori welfare. The local Maori Councils which had been instituted in 1900 and which in many districts had at first been only lukewarm in their efforts, began to do more to help.

The Census of 1901 had shown 43,143 Maoris; by 1911 the total had increased to 49,844. Clearly the gloomy prophecies of ultimate extinction had been disproved, and under the guidance of leaders from among themselves the Maori people had taken new heart.

11
Acceptance of Responsibility

THE MAORIS OF TARANAKI, just beginning to emerge from the years of despair and isolation, had shown little interest in politics. To them Parliament was a pakeha institution which had been their enemy in the past and even the fact that they had the right to vote in the election of a Maori member meant little to them for the overwhelming numbers of the Tainui tribes of the Waikato had always ensured that the Western Maori member was from that district.

The crucial moment came when Te Kahupukoro, heading a Taranaki delegation to Timi Kara in Wellington, was advised by the latter in cryptic terms to seek out a young man to act as his eyes, in other words to represent Taranaki in Parliament.

At a meeting held at Ketemarae Pa near Normanby, Maui Pomare agreed to accept nomination and after tactful negotiation with King Rata and the Waikato tribes sufficient support was gained to ensure his election. In 1912 he took his seat in Parliament as an Independent but within a few months had decided to support the Reform party and was included in Massey's cabinet as Representative of the Native Race with responsibility for the Cook Islands. Both Ngata and Te Rangihiroa were by this time also in Parliament, Ngata having been elected first in 1906 and Te Rangihiroa in 1909 but as both supported the Liberal party, together with Timi Kara, neither was eligible for Cabinet rank under Massey.

The first major task which fell to Maui Pomare was to attempt a solution of the complicated land problems of his own people in Taranaki. In 1880 the West Coast Settlement Act had reserved 187,000 acres as the absolute property of the original Maori inhabitants, but at the same time the reserved areas were vested in the Public Trustee with power to lease whatever land was not required for Maori use. Moreover even the Maori owners had to pay rent for the lands allotted to them by the Public Trustee. All rents received, from whatever source, were to be divided equally among the members of the tribes to which the lands were reserved.

No doubt the regulations were intended to protect the Maori from the temptation to sell his land without thought for the future, as had taken place in so many parts of the country; but to the Maori the fact which overshadowed everything else was that he had become a rent-paying tenant on his own ancestral land and even his right to occupy was insecure, for was not the Public Trustee entitled to terminate that right if he chose? In conflict with an impersonal Government department, the Maori felt bewildered and helpless.

But an even more bitter blow was dealt him in 1892. By the West Coast Settlement Reserves Act, passed by Parliament without investigating Maori opinion in the matter, pakeha tenants were given the right to convert their term leases into ones with a perpetual right of renewal, provided that they availed themselves of the opportunity before

4th November 1900. By that date only 18,000 acres remained on term leases. Although the Maori was receiving the rents from the leased property the opportunity to use the greater part of his land had been taken from him for ever.

It was doubtful whether he could regain possession even of the land held on term leases, for a clause in the Act specified that up to £5 an acre should be paid to compensate for improvements if the land were re-leased or reverted to the owners; and the Maori was in no position to raise the considerable sum needed to pay that compensation.

By 1912 the leases were almost due to expire and the situation clearly required urgent action. Pomare, supported by the Maori Union, threw himself into the struggle and finally after long months of hard bargaining between the Union and the Taranaki settlers a compromise was reached in 1913. The settlers were granted an extension of their leases for a further ten years; at the end of that period the land would revert to the Maori owners – and the Public Trustee was authorised to advance whatever funds should prove necessary to enable the Maoris to pay the compensation for improvements.

The wisdom of Timi Kara's advice to Te Kahupukoro had become apparent; without the young man to act as his eyes in Parliament it is doubtful if even these last fragments of the Taranaki inheritance could have been salvaged.

In contrast with those of Ngata and Pomare, Te Rangihiroa's political career was brief. As a Government Health Officer he had gained great respect among the Maori people of Northland through his devoted toil during an alarming epidemic of small-pox; accordingly, when the death of Hone Heke, a relative of the redoubtable chief of earlier times, had left the Northern Maori seat vacant in 1909, it was felt that none was better fitted than Te Rangihiroa to be his successor. He represented the Northern electorate until the end of 1914; in the following February he left as Medical Officer with the First Maori Contingent to go overseas in the First World War.

The major achievements of Apirana Ngata were yet to come, but already his personality and ability were beginning to make their impact on Parliament. In 1907 he was appointed to a Royal Commission with Sir Robert Stout, the Chief Justice, to investigate the whole question of the use and sale of Maori land; two years later the report of the Commission was presented and its recommendations were incorporated in the Native Land Act of 1909.

From that date Maori land could not be sold except through Maori Land Councils; the elders of the tribes were again placed in a position where they could exercise their authority to control the sale of tribal land, and some tribes with a clearer eye to the future held fast to the land which they still retained. But in spite of Ngata's hopes not all were so prudent. Within the next ten years three million acres more were sold.

The Young Maori Party leaders fully understood the views of both Maori and pakeha in the land conflicts of the past and Ngata was a fully qualified and able lawyer. He saw clearly that unused Maori land, derelict and weed-infested, was a continuous irritation to pakeha farmers, not only to those who felt indignant at the waste of potentially good land when they themselves were unable to enlarge their farms, but also to those whose farms were adversely affected through the spread of plant and animal pests from the neglected areas. Ngata stressed the point continually that only the lands which the Maori people themselves would usefully occupy would ultimately remain in their possession; and proceeded in a practical way to demonstrate that the Maori could use his land efficiently.

But first of all the complications of title which had arisen since 1865 had to be unravelled. The granting of individual titles to fractions of tribal land had led in the past to minute fragmentation of blocks of land among the descendants of the original title-holders. One man might own many small sections scattered over a wide area; none would be large enough for him to farm economically and as a result all would be neglected.

In an attempt to solve the problem of fragmentation a clause was inserted in the 1909 Act allowing for consolidation of interests, whereby a block could be re-subdivided, allotting each owner a single farm equal in area to the total of the fragments which he previously had held. Although the consolidation scheme appeared to be a promising one, which many owners were pleased to adopt, it has proved to be cumbersome in operation and moreover, does not offer a final solution of the problem, for the death of the owner of a consolidated farm immediately starts a new process of fragmentation.

However even the partial success of the new scheme showed the Maori people that they had a leader who understood their problems and was striving to solve them. What was more, it was clear that his mana was sufficiently high among the pakehas to win support in the Government itself.

From 1912 Pomare was given responsibility for the Cook Islands; after four years the status of his position was raised by his being designated Minister for the Cook Islands. For the first time since the proclamation of a British Protectorate over the islands in 1888, the welfare of the Pacific Maoris was to be in the hands of a man of the same people as themselves, one whose genealogies led back to the same ancestors whose names they themselves held in veneration.

Little has so far been found to date the earliest settlement of the Cook Islands but it appears that Polynesians were established there at least from the time of the first arrivals in New Zealand. Probably the majority of the settlers came from Tahiti but there are signs of influences from Samoa also. Legend tells of a division of the island of Rarotonga between a Samoan party led by Karika and a Tahitian group under Tangiia.

As might be expected from their geographical position, the Cook Islands were less isolated than New Zealand during the centuries after 1350; certainly there were occasional contacts with Tahiti. When pakehas reached Rarotonga they found the inhabitants familiar with Tahitian religion.

Within the main Cook Group voyaging was frequent. There are tales of war between the inhabitants of Atiu, Mauke, Mitiaro and Manuae, of Aitutakian invasions of Rarotonga, and of a raid on Mangaia from an island to the north-east. It is known, too, that the people of Mauke used to obtain fish, birds' eggs and feathers from Maria Island (Nurotu) two hundred miles away from their home.

Although included in the Cook Islands Dependency for administrative purposes, the Northern Cooks – Rakaanga, Pukapuka, Nassau, Manihiki, and Tongareva (Penrhyn) – form a separate group, and there is little indication of contacts between the two groups. The affinities of the Northern Cooks were with Samoa and Tonga rather than with Tahiti; Pukapuka is considered to have been settled from Tonga about 1300 A.D.

The first pakeha visitor recorded in the Cook Islands proper was Captain Cook in 1773, and various others called from time to time after that year without making much impact on the life of the people until, after fifty years of intermittent contact with the outside world, the islanders saw the first mission station established in Rarotonga.

The London Mission Society, an interdenominational organisation in which Congregationalists, Anglicans, Methodists and Presbyterians were associated, was founded in England in 1795, and the following year its first missionaries were sent to Tahiti. For many years their work was restricted to the Society Group but eventually the mission was sufficiently firmly established to send both pakeha and Tahitian missionaries to the Cook Islands. With the spread of Christianity tribal conflict died out, and under missionary influence the chiefs imposed a code of laws which were strictly enforced until some modifications were made after a British protectorate was proclaimed.

The New Zealand Government exercised control through a Resident, the first of whom in 1891 set up an elected parliament and an Executive Council of arikis, with the senior ariki, Queen Makea of Avarua, as head of the Government.

The people of the Northern Cook Islands, which carry only a sixth of the population of the combined group, were converted to Christianity by Polynesian missionaries from the London Missionary Society centre in Rarotonga. Apart from the introduction of Christianity and a certain limited amount of trade, the pakeha made little impact on the lives of the Northern Cook Islanders, except for a disastrous blow suffered in 1863, when many people were carried off from Pukapuka and Penrhyn in a raid by Peruvian slave-traders.

Although the whole of the Cook Islands became New Zealand territory in 1901 little interest was taken in their people until responsibility for this group of Maoris came into Pomare's hands. As Maori Health Officer, he had made a six-month survey of conditions in the islands in 1905 and he was well aware that, as far as health was concerned, the Cook Islanders were in exactly the same position as his own people in New Zealand. Pakeha diseases had ravaged the islands. On Rarotonga alone an estimated population of six thousand in 1827 had been reduced to little more than two thousand by 1901.

Pomare's recommendations for improvements were carried out as far as was possible with the limited funds which were available but it was not until he became a Cabinet Minister that he was in a position to make the drastic changes which the situation warranted.

In 1915, after many months of preparation, he was able to gain Parliamentary consent to a bill which covered almost every aspect of life in the Cook Islands; henceforth education, government and health services all had a firm foundation on which to build. By the time Pomare gave up office after many years of devotion to the welfare of the people, the Cook Islanders themselves were well aware of what he had achieved. No name held greater mana in the islands than that of Maui Pomare.

Each island by this time had an effective Council to order its own local affairs. In general government officials and arikis were Council members by right of office; other members were nominated or elected and on Rarotonga the small pakeha community was also allotted one elected representative. Government schools had been established on the principal islands of the main Cook group while with the aid of a Government grant the London Mission Society had opened schools with trained Polynesian teachers in the Northern Cooks. A technical school was in operation on Rarotonga, at Avarua.

As was to be expected, Pomare had striven hard to improve health conditions. Good water supplies had been provided for each island, the work of the resident Health Officers in Rarotonga had been supplemented by sending trained Polynesian nurses to the other islands and, as in New Zealand, doctrines of hygiene were preached unceasingly.

Already the improvement in health was beginning to show as a new generation grew up. The total population which had been 8,655 in 1911, had become 10,082 in 1926, and was increasing at more than double the rate it was when Pomare took the Cook Islands into his charge.

With the increasing population on the islands it was essential that the major source of income – the production of tropical fruit – should increase in proportion; Pomare did everything possible to develop the fruit trade, encouraging the islanders not only to produce more but also to export some of it themselves – a move which was not altogether popular with the pakeha trading community.

Moreover, he was determined that the unhappy land situation in New Zealand should not be duplicated in the islands; the principle that only the Polynesian inhabitants should own land was strictly guarded. No land was to be sold or mortgaged and no leases could last for more than 60 years.

By the time that Maui Pomare's work for his Polynesian kindred came to an end another Maori, Dr Edward Pohau Ellison, had begun a career of service in the islands.

12
The Wider View

THE YEAR 1893 was a momentous one in the story of the Maori people; it was the year in which Timi Kara was elected to represent a pakeha electorate and Apirana Ngata qualified for a University degree. Each had shown that he could meet the challenge of pakeha society on its own ground and succeed in what he attempted.

As we have seen, others quickly followed. Maui Pomare, Te Rangihiroa and Tutere Wirepa qualified in medicine and it became clear that the Maori was capable of taking his rightful place in the leadership of the New Zealand people as a whole.

When war came in 1914 a Maori contingent was soon in action overseas, first on Gallipoli and then in France; Maori and pakeha, equally New Zealanders, fought together as comrades under the same flag, sharing dangers and hardship in an atmosphere of mutual respect.

Te Rangihiroa left with the Contingent in February 1915 as Medical Officer, then after the move to France he became a combatant officer with the rank of Major and was appointed second in command of the battalion. Finally, in 1918, he was transferred to medical duties again both at the front and in the New Zealand hospital.

After the war he returned to health work among his own people but his special ability in anthropology soon began to attract attention far beyond the bounds of New Zealand An invitation to join the staff of the Bernice P. Bishop Museum in Honolulu was accepted and from 1927 he was engaged in research work among the Polynesian peoples throughout the Pacific.

By the time of his death in 1951 he had gained world-wide renown as an authoritative scholar and scientist and had been created K.C.M.G.; Yale University in the United States had appointed him Professor of Anthropology, and for many years he had been Director of the Bishop Museum.

His books are his memorial, and embody his alert and genial personality. Through his painstaking research he gave to the world as no one – pakeha or Maori – had done before, a full and authentic picture of Maori society against the background of the widespread culture of the Polynesian people.

The achievements of Maui Pomare among the Maori people of New Zealand as Medical Officer and among the Cook Islanders as a member of Cabinet had brought general recognition of his ability. In 1923 the Prime Minister made him Minister of Health; the welfare of both pakeha and Maori were now to be in his hands and he entered upon his task with the same vigour and sense of duty as he had shown in narrower fields.

Although he held office as Minister of Health for only three years, Pomare was able to make far-reaching reforms, especially in providing better facilities for the treatment of the mentally ill. On relinquishing his position he devoted his energies to a project which he had had before his mind for many years – the care of lepers.

Leprosy is not a disease introduced by the pakeha. Under the names of ngerengere, tuwhenua or tuhawaiki, it is known to have appeared from time to time among the Maori people from early times and according to legend it was brought to Northland by two canoes, Moekakara and Te Wakatuwhenua. Possibly both names represent the same canoe. Nothing is known of the leprosy canoes except their names and where they made landfall; not even the names of their commanders are remembered. Where the disease came from is difficult to determine for there appears to have been no leprosy in other parts of Polynesia until it was introduced last century by Chinese and other labourers from Asia.

However although it was uncommon, there were several sufferers from leprosy both in New Zealand and the islands when Pomare turned his attention to this dreaded disease. In the early years of the century Pomare called for action in the case of the lepers in New Zealand, both pakeha and Maori, who at that time were not segregated nor given effective medical treatment. Eventually his voice was heeded and Quail Island in Lyttelton Harbour became a centre for their treatment.

In the Cook Islands there was equal neglect; on Penrhyn Island there was a small colony of lepers in voluntary isolation but there was no provision for regular medical treatment and living conditions were appalling.

There had been a leper station on Makogai Island in Fiji since 1911; Pomare finally brought about an agreement whereby patients from other islands of the South Pacific could be accepted at Makogai and in 1926 a Government vessel was sent round the islands to collect lepers. The complete success of this voluntary transfer – for there was no power to enforce the removal of patients – was in no small measure due to the mana of Maui Pomare and Pohau Ellison, then Chief Medical Officer at Rarotonga, both of whom were in the official party aboard the transfer ship.

Edward Pohau Ellison, who was born at Waikanae in

1884, was a grandson of Te Ika-i-raua, daughter of the chief Te Whati of the Ngati-tama tribe and her pakeha husband Thomas Ellison. On his mother's side he was a grandson of Nikuru Taiaroa of Otakou, who had also married a pakeha, Edward Weller.

Pohau's father, Raniera Ellison, who fully realised the value of education had encouraged one son, Thomas, to study law and on the latter's death in 1904 he hoped that Pohau, who was then at Te Aute College, would take up the same profession. But Pohau Ellison had decided on a different career and following in the footsteps of Te Rangihiroa and Tutere Wirepa he eventually graduated in medicine at Otago University.

In 1919 he was appointed Resident Medical Officer and Commissioner for Niue Island which had been transferred to New Zealand control at about the same time as the Cook Islands, but placed under separate administration in 1903.

Niue has a history of settlement from both Tonga and Samoa and appears to have been inhabited by Polynesians for over a thousand years. Captain Cook had visited Niue but pakehas, whether traders or missionaries, were not welcomed by the Niuean people and it was not until 1861 that the first pakeha missionary was allowed to settle on the island. In the meantime the islanders had become Christians under the influence of a Samoan mission teacher, Paulo, who had landed in 1849.

At the request of the Niuean people they were taken under British protection in 1888 and later local government was organised by the setting up of an Island Council. The heads of families were the leaders of the people for there were no hereditary chiefs on Niue.

After three years on Niue, Pohau Ellison took up a similar appointment in the Chatham Islands returning to New Zealand to take a post-graduate course in tropical diseases.

The course of his life's work was now clear and apart from a four-year period when he was recalled to take the position of Director of Maori Hygiene, Pohau Ellison was Chief Medical Officer of the Cook Islands until 1945 as well as being Commissioner of the High Court there for thirteen years.

On his retirement from official life he returned to New Zealand to practice medicine in South Taranaki, where pakeha and Maori alike respected the ability, kindliness and Christian humility of this man who had devoted his life to the welfare of others.

By 1921 it was clear for all to see that the Maori people, under their own leaders and with the friendly co-operation of the pakeha, had emerged from the shadows. Their numbers had increased in one generation from 42,000 in 1891 to nearly 53,000 in 1921; Maoris had gained outstanding academic qualifications, positions of authority in the government of New Zealand and high esteem overseas.

But although the people as a whole had achieved much and there had been a vast improvement in Maori relations with the pakeha, a black cloud still hung over many of the tribes: the shadow of a great injustice, the confiscation of their land. Parliament was petitioned again and again, deputations pressed their claims, ministers were urged to act in the name of justice, a party of Maoris visited England in the hope of putting their case before the king; but all was without avail and the frustrated people began to despair of any redress.

In fact the Government was not unsympathetic, but it was in a very difficult constitutional position over the whole matter of the Maori claims, and it says much for the goodwill and honesty of purpose of Gordon Coates, the Prime Minister, that he was prepared to set up a tribunal before which the Government itself was to be the defendant.

This was the Royal Commission of 1926. Maui Pomare had realised that individual appeals were useless and that the only way in which success was at all possible was for able lawyers to present a carefully prepared and fully documented case before such a body.

The Commission, which was instructed to inquire into the causes of the Taranaki Wars and fix the responsibility for the conflict, came to the conclusion that the wars had arisen out of the Waitara purchase and that "the Government was wrong in declaring war against the natives for the purpose of establishing the supposed rights of the Crown under that purchase. The natives were treated as rebels and war declared against them before they had engaged in rebellion of any kind."

It was "an unjust and unholy war" and the Maoris should not have been punished by the confiscation of any of their land. The Waikato tribes had been technically guilty of rebellion but the Commission noted that the innocent had been punished by confiscation and the guilty left untouched.

Finally, the Commission recommended that compensation should be paid by the State to the tribes which had lost their lands; this recommendation was promptly carried out and the Government undertook to establish Maori Trust Boards to receive and administer all compensation payments.

A sum of £5000 is paid annually to the Taranaki Maori Trust Board and used in furthering the welfare of the Maori people in that area. In all conscience it is a small enough sum as compensation for the 462,000 acres which were finally confiscated but many factors must be taken into account.

The payment is not being made by those actually responsible for the wrong done, nor is the sum paid to those who directly suffered but to their heirs. The Commission admitted that it was difficult, if not impossible, to arrive at a satisfactory conclusion as to the value of the land at the time of its confiscation. The point which is important is that a past offence had been atoned for; the Maoris no longer had a sense of grievance in that they had been wrongfully branded as rebels.

What had been done in the past could not be undone but

the future lay before them and the Government had shown, not only by words but also by deeds, that Maori and pakeha were to walk together as equals on the road ahead.

But the iron had gone more deeply into the soul of the Waikato tribes. Remaining proudly aloof, their leaders scornfully rejected the proffered compensation, declaring that only the return of part at least of their lost lands could make amends. Fortunately they had among them one who had the clear insight to realise the situation in all its aspects, that remarkable woman, Te Puea Herangi, Princess Te Puea, whose mother was the eldest daughter of King Tawhiao.

She saw clearly that her people by their own action were hurting only themselves. Brooding over the past was crippling them for the future and she set herself with courage and determination to show the Waikato tribes where their destiny lay. Ultimately they, too, accepted compensation and the Tainui Trust Board was established.

By 1960 there were ten Maori Trust Boards administering funds built up from various sources including the compensation money for land confiscations. Their actions are subject to the approval of the Minister of Maori Affairs but their membership is wholly Maori and they have wide powers to use their funds for the benefit of the tribe that each represents. The promotion of health, social and economic welfare, education and vocational training, all come within the scope of their aims.

Given the opportunity the Maori is using his money wisely and well.

Maori Trust Boards 1960

Administering compensation payments for the confiscated land:

Tainui (£5000 a year in perpetuity plus £1000 a year for 45 years).

Taranaki (£5000 a year in perpetuity).
Whakatohea (£20,000).

Administering payments concerning ownership of Taupo and the Rotorua lakes:

Arawa (£6000 a year in perpetuity).
Tuwharetoa (£3000 a year in perpetuity plus half fishing licence fees above £3000 a year).

Administering payments for land bought by the Crown:

Aorangi (£22,500).
Ngaitahu (£10,000 a year for 30 years).
Taitokerau (£47,000).
Wairoa (£20,000).

Administering certain land income and proceeds from a communal enterprise at Te Kao:

Aupouri (No payment by Crown).

The Ngati-porou people were in a unique position among all the tribes of New Zealand. Their tribal territory was isolated by bush and mountain barriers, pakeha settlement had come late, and the numbers of settlers were small, so that the amount of land sold was not excessive. Moreover Ngati-porou had taken no part in the Taranaki and Waikato wars so that no land had been lost by confiscation. The missionary influence was still strong and pakehas such as the Williams family, who fully understood the Maori point of view, were held in high respect.

Accordingly, Ngati-porou entered the twentieth century as a united people with a strong tribal spirit and were fortunate in having extremely able and far-sighted leaders.

Ropata Wahawaha and his companion in arms during the Te Kooti campaigns, Mokena Kohere, were firmly opposed to further sales of tribal land and when the mana of Ropata passed to Paratene Ngata and eventually to the latter's son, Apirana, the same policy was continued.

Apirana Ngata's alert legal mind was soon grappling with the problem of how the land which the tribe fortunately still possessed could be used to the best advantage. He saw clearly that leadership must come from the Maori people themselves and that control could be exerted most effectively in an atmosphere of tribal loyalty and unity.

The Maori must acquire what he needed from pakeha culture without surrendering what was of value in his own traditions. The man who leaps recklessly overboard is no more likely to reach the shore than the one who clings desperately to the sinking ship; the wise man remains on board until the life-boat is launched. In the communal spirit of the tribe, the language, crafts and traditions of the Maori people, Ngata saw the life-boat which could bring his people to safety.

Apirana Ngata's first scheme skilfully blended Maori custom and pakeha law by the simple measure of forming a group of landowners into an incorporated company which then elected a committee to control its lands. As the committee desired it could then either lease its properties or select a manager to farm them. Although at first it was often considered wise to give experienced pakeha farm-managers the responsibility of running incorporated farms, the numbers of Maori managers steadily increased.

Most of the work on the farms was done by the actual owners, who thus enjoyed the benefits of a co-operative organisation by receiving wages as employees and also sharing in the profits as shareholders.

Ngata's second scheme was for the consolidation of fragmented land. Although it was found after a number of years that the method was cumbersome and the result insufficiently permanent, consolidation did much to stimulate the Maori people to use land which had lain idle and the example of Ngati-porou was soon followed by other tribes.

It was clear that Ngata's two methods for developing Maori land for the benefit of its owners were workable; the people were keen to learn and willing to work; the difficulties due to fragmentation of land were being overcome. But no land development scheme can be operated efficiently without adequate capital, and Ngata's next problem was to find that capital.

Timi Kara and the Young Maori Party had pointed out that, although pakeha settlers were able to obtain Government assistance, the Maori farmer attempting to farm his own land had no such advantage. Private organisations too, were reluctant to advance loans to Maoris. Ngata felt that the only way to win recognition of Maori needs for financial assistance from the Government was to show what the Maori himself could achieve by self-reliance and use of his own funds.

In 1921 the Native Trust Office was brought into existence to administer various Maori reserves and funds which had formerly been controlled by the Public Trustee and the Native Trustee was given power to assist Maori farming or other enterprises. Five years later the same authority to lend money to Maoris on mortgage was given to the Native Land Boards. Thus the Maori was enabled to use his own money to good purpose.

The success of the Ngati-porou schemes began to attract the attention of other tribes. By 1928 the whole of the Urewera land had been consolidated, the Arawa soon followed by consolidating the Maketu coastal area, and in a few years the Northland and King Country people had decided to follow suit.

By this time Ngati-porou were embarking on fresh ventures in which the tribal spirit could be enlisted to support modern developments. Sheep farming had been their first enterprise; in 1923 the more intensive dairy farming was undertaken and a co-operative butter factory was established followed quickly by a trading firm, the Waiapu Farmers' Co-operative Company.

Financial help came at first from sympathetic pakeha families, and later banks and the Government advanced funds. The key men – pakeha or Maori – were chosen with care, and the enthusiasm and will to work of the Ngati-porou people brought the success that they deserved.

At the end of 1928 a change of government brought Ngata to office as Minister of Native Affairs; the next year Parliament passed the Native Land Development and Settlement Act, whereby for the first time the Government itself was to provide money to develop Maori lands and train Maoris to be efficient farmers. With his customary energy Ngata began to push his schemes ahead.

Among the Arawa people he had already found strong sympathy for his views and in Henry Taiporutu Mitchell and Henry Te Reiwhati Vercoe, leading men in the Arawa confederation of tribes, he had staunch supporters who never ceased to advocate land development on the lines propounded by Ngata.

Mitchell, who was born in Rotorua in 1877, joined the Lands and Survey Department at the age of 17 and by 1908 had become Director of Native Surveys. After twenty years with the department he entered private practice, but returned in 1926 to the Government service as Consolidation Officer, Surveyor and Welfare Officer in the Native Department. When he died in 1944 he had earned the respect of Maori and pakeha alike for the active part he had taken in public affairs not only to help the Maori people but for the good of the whole community.

Henry Vercoe, who was born in 1884 at the historic Arawa settlement of Maketu, died in 1962 after a long career of service to the Maori people. He was a man of foresight, courage and vigour. Before he was 16 he had enlisted for the Boer War from which he returned with the award of the D.C.M. When war came in 1914 he again went overseas, took part in the campaigns in Gallipoli and France with the Maori Contingent and gained the further distinction of the D.S.O. In the Second World War, with the rank of Major he commanded a training camp for Maori troops in New Zealand.

It was most unfortunate that Major Vercoe did not live to attend the memorable first meeting of the Dominion Maori Council, for it was largely due to his enthusiasm that discussions on the formation of such a body were carried forward to a successful conclusion.

With the approval and active support of the Arawa leaders, Ngata began plans for the settlement of the 10,000-acre Horohoro block south-west of Rotorua. In 1930 the pioneers moved on to the area; among the Ngati-tuara Arawa settlers who had had little farming experience were 14 Kahungunu from Wairoa, accustomed to work on the land and so able to give the settlement the benefit of their experience.

The land was a bleak wilderness when the first furrow was turned, money was available in only limited amounts – for by this time New Zealand was in the grip of the great depression – and life was so hard that at times the future must have seemed hopeless. But the Ngati-tuara and Kahungunu settlers persevered with their efforts until the pumice scrub-land was transformed into prosperous farms. Once again Ngata's formula of careful selection of leaders, communal effort and hard work had proved successful.

Until his resignation as Minister of Native Affairs in 1933 Ngata, by this time Sir Apirana for he had been knighted in 1927, exercised a very real and personal control over the land schemes which he had initiated, and by the time that he gave up office the foundations of future development had been laid.

In the 17 years before his death in 1950, he was able to see his plans adopted widely throughout the country until over 300,000 acres of what had been useless land was being farmed by Maori settlers.

13
Maoritanga

"KIA MAU KI TO KOUTOU MAORITANGA" (Retain your Maori heritage – remain Maori) said Timi Kara at a time when the Maori was standing hesitant and bewildered in a changing world – and fortunately his listeners paid heed to his words.

Maoritanga has meant different things at different times and in varying places. To some it has meant a rejection of things pakeha, an attempt to withdraw into the past, a renunciation of progress; to others it has meant little more than treasuring a sentimental dream of an unreal Maori past while making every effort to become pakeha.

But Timi Kara and the men of the Young Maori Party were essentially realists. To try to live in the past was to show unrealistic defeatism, but to abandon the heritage of their ancestors completely in the attempt to acquire pakeha culture was like starting to cross a dangerous mountain river without a rope.

There was much in the culture of the past which had outlived its usefulness and no longer needed to be retained;

it was futile to use a stone adze when steel was ready to hand, but there was still a place for the arts and crafts, the skills of weaving and carving, blending Maori tradition and pakeha techniques, the emotive rhythm of the poi dance, the action song and the haka. The legends and traditions of the Maori past, the tales of courage and high adventure, afford a background for the literature of the future. The marae, and the meeting-house on which the highest skill has been lavished, can still play their part in a modern world, and the tangi not only honours the dead but also brings closer bonds of union among the living.

The traditional arts and crafts of any human community are unique. They may have had a common origin with those of similar groups, they may have been derived in part from alien cultures, yet nevertheless the community which possesses them has made them essentially its own, rejecting what was not in tune with its philosophy of life and at times altering what has been borrowed until all signs of its origin are lost. So the arts and crafts are clearly interwoven with the corporate life of the people, developed by them and binding them together with pride in their heritage.

But cultures evolve. Maori flute music with its limited range of notes has been abandoned for pakeha tunes, some of which have become so thoroughly accepted as Maori melodies that few realise their origin. With his good ear for music the Maori quickly took up new melodies, played them on the concertina and in later times the guitar, sang them in his own language, and in so doing made them his own.

When Ngata began to arouse the interest of his people in reviving their fast-vanishing arts his own tribe was one which still retained a strong carving tradition. Styles varied in different parts of New Zealand but, as the result of the employment of skilled Ngati-porou by other tribes, certain features of design formerly distinctive of the East Coast have become widespread.

There are few tribes which do not possess a whare whakairo,

a meeting-house of which they can be proud, with its intricately carved front, its interior with painted rafter designs and skilfully patterned tukutuku wall panels. The meeting-house is the focus of community life and where the community spirit is strong it is expressed in the desire for a worthy whare whakairo.

With the revival of carving there came also an upsurge of interest in the arts of weaving and plaiting. Ngati-porou and Arawa did much to show that the Maori of the twentieth century could still feel an inner satisfaction in pursuing the arts of his ancestors; soon the Waikato people followed under the guidance of Te Puea Herangi.

Princess Te Puea was born at Whatiwhatihoe in 1884; she received a pakeha education, partly in Auckland, then devoted her life to the welfare of the Waikato people. To the mana of her position was added a clear-sightedness and strength of character which were to prove of inestimable benefit to her people who had entered the twentieth century dispossessed of their land and sullenly resentful of the pakeha.

In politics, in education, in health and in farming, Te Puea's driving force and enthusiasm led the way and, reluctantly at first, her people followed. She wore down the resistance of conservative-minded elders who at first refused to accept compensation for the loss of their confiscated lands and eventually the Tainui Trust Board was established.

Meanwhile under her guidance the Waikato people had begun to adopt Ngata's methods of farming on such land as still remained to them.

However in Te Puea's view the regeneration of the tribes could only be finally accomplished if the status of the Maori King were established. She realised that a king in exile might command loyalty but could never gain the real prestige of his position until he lived in a worthy home on his own ancestral land. Accordingly with a handful of devoted followers she set about acquiring such land as was needed for the purpose.

Finally through accepting scrub-cutting and road-making contracts, in fact any work that was available, however arduous, they had saved sufficient funds to take the first step. Fifteen acres of land was bought at Ngaruawahia, the former capital of Te Puea's ancestors, a new pa – Turangawaewae – was built, strict attention being paid to rules of health, and the skill of craftsmen was enlisted in the erection of Mahinarangi, the beautiful meeting-house.

As the years passed more buildings rose so that Maori traditions of hospitality could be worthily observed, ancient skills were revived or developed and the influence of the princess was exerted to encourage pride of race and pride of achievement wherever Tainui people were to be found.

The Waikato people had found their soul and long before her death in 1952 Princess Te Puea's outstanding personality had come to be regarded with respect by both Maori and pakeha.

In one respect all Maori leaders were in agreement: the Maori language must be retained. Whatever its distant future might be the value of the language as a unifying bond between tribes and a practical reminder of Maoritanga was clearly recognised. Taking a still wider view, the modern Maori is aware of kinship with the peoples of the Pacific whose languages he can understand and even in distant Malaya he hears echoes of familiar words.

In the ancient language there undoubtedly were dialectal differences but as tribal isolation broke down the dialects merged into what is now virtually one language. There are some variations still as between east and west but tribal intermingling and the influence of printed Maori, especially of the Maori Bible, have been powerful levelling factors.

The language, however, has changed in another way. Ancient Maori was fully adequate as a means of communication and a medium for emotional expression in the culture in which it had grown. But the culture of the pakeha brought with it much that was new, both in material things and in mental concepts, and the reaction of the speakers of Maori was identical with that of other peoples in a similar situation. Words were adopted freely from English to express what was formerly unknown. The pronunciation of such words was altered to bring them into line with Maori speech traditions, so that very many speakers of Maori at the present time are scarcely aware of what has been borrowed and what has not.

Only dwellers in very remote districts would find the old Maori language sufficient for all purposes; those who are in the main stream of New Zealand life would immediately feel hampered and restricted if all words of English origin were denied them.

It is obvious therefore that to speak only Maori is to be cut off from New Zealand life as a whole; yet to learn both languages is to begin education with a handicap which for the great majority is difficult to overcome. Only the Maori who thoroughly masters English can feel competent to take the full part in the community that his ability entitles him to. It is not sufficient to read, write and speak English. What is essential is to learn to think in English and here at once can be seen a major problem in Maori education of the present day.

Only a limited number of people in a population become really proficient in two languages. Sir Apirana Ngata was one who fully achieved that aim but most people of average ability, Maori or pakeha, find that learning a second language thoroughly retards progress in all other subjects.

When Maori State primary schools were established in the nineteenth century the advantage to a Maori of being able to speak English was recognised and it was laid down that instruction should be in English. At the same time it was tacitly assumed by the Government that the Maori language – and perhaps the Maori people themselves – were doomed to rapid extinction.

The situation now is vastly different. The Maori language

has a part to play in bringing together the people who speak it in giving the Maori pride in his ancestry and confidence to face the future. Clearly the language will remain for many years to come, and therefore most Maoris at some stage have to face the problem of bilingualism either consciously or subconsciously.

The difficulty has been met in various ways. Some have chosen to abandon Maori completely; others speak English as their usual language but have retained sufficient Maori to enable them to take their place in gatherings where Maori is spoken; others again use English self-consciously as a foreign tongue with which they are never really at ease.

Only those who have gained a mastery over both tongues are in a position to guide policy in the future.

The period of the nineteen-twenties was one of growing awareness of Maoritanga by both Maori and pakeha. The Government, which had shown its willingness to make amends for past injustice and help re-establish Maori mana, set up in 1926 a Board of Arts and Crafts to encourage the revival of traditional skills. A school of Maori carving was established in Rotorua and within a few years several hundred young Maoris had pursued studies there, acquired competence in the art and carried their knowledge and skill back to their own people.

In the Maori schools too there were developments. As D. G. Ball, a former inspector of Maori schools, pointed out, until 1931 the Education Department "persevered with a policy that attempted to divorce the Maori from every aspect of his culture, whether good or bad." The prevailing attitude was that the school existed solely to give the pupil a pakeha education; he could acquire his Maori culture at home.

However, slowly at first, changes were introduced in the years preceding the Second World War. Maori arts and crafts, the history, poems and legends of their own people came to be included in the curricula of Maori schools;

moreover, with the encouragement and support of their own leaders, young Maori men and women began to come forward to learn the pakeha's methods, to train as teachers and then to work for their own people in Maori schools.

It was also recognised that for many Maoris a purely academic education was of little real value; accordingly greater emphasis was laid on acquiring practical knowledge and skills closely linked with the needs of the community.

From being an isolated outpost of pakeha culture in a Maori world, the school became an integral part of social life. The school began to play its part in helping the adults of the district; they in turn became increasingly interested and co-operative in the work of the school.

By 1939 Maoritanga had become a vital force for progress in the Maori world.

14
Religion in the New Century

IT HAS BEEN SEEN that with the conflicts of the middle of the nineteenth century there came a wave of doubt and mistrust of the pakeha, a wave which in some districts made strong inroads into Maori Christian congregations. But eventually, after the first shock had spent its force, the wave ebbed away and many of those whose faith had wavered returned to their former religions.

However the Ringatu followers of Te Kooti's teachings held their ground in the Urewera, and in South Taranaki Te Whiti and Tohu preached their doctrine of non-cooperation and peaceful resistence to pakeha ways.

Te Whiti died in 1907; although many of his followers slowly became satisfied that the teachings of the Young Maori Party held hope for the future, there were hundreds throughout Northland, the Bay of Plenty, the Waikato and the South Island who were still suspicious of anything connected with the pakeha. Even their own enlightened leaders found it difficult to convince them that the only way for the Maori people to survive was to acquire pakeha knowledge and come to terms with the pakeha society in which they found themselves.

The gap appeared to be too wide to bridge; why make the effort and risk failure? And they sank back into apathetic dreaming, waiting for the Messiah whom Te Whiti had foretold. The disastrous influenza epidemic of 1918, in which 1200 Maoris died – a very high proportion compared with the number of pakeha deaths – plunged them still further into despair.

It was at this moment, when life seemed to have reached its lowest ebb, that they became aware that their long-awaited prophet was among them.

Tahupotiki Wiremu Ratana was the man. He was born in 1873 at Parewanui Pa, near the mouth of the Rangitikei River, and from his boyhood had been greatly influenced by his aunt, Mere Rikiriki, a prophet and faith-healer who saw in her nephew the promised Messiah. In 1918 convinced by a vision that he was the Mangai, the Mouthpiece of God, Ratana determined to lead his people away from super-stition and ignorance to faith in God, to heal their bodies and give them a purpose in life.

The prophet's ministry of faith-healing quickly made his name known throughout the country. Maori and pakeha flocked to him to be cured, devoted followers who had come to him for bodily or spiritual healing decided to remain near him, and a village of hastily built dwellings sprang up round his house.

Ratana had no intention of founding a new church; his aim was primarily that of a religious teacher to quicken faith and hope in a people who were in danger of losing both, but by 1925 it began to appear that unless it made a separate path for itself the driving force of his movement would be lost. Accordingly in that year the prophet reluctantly broke with the other Christian denominations and the Ratana Church as such came into existence. Three years later the new organisation was visibly consolidated by the building of the Temple.

The Ratana Church is deeply rooted in Christianity but it is a Maori Christianity and satisfies the desire for Maoritanga for which Ratana's people had been groping fruitlessly in the years before his ministry began. An indication of the new church's strength was given by the census of 1926 in which it was shown to have 11,567 adherents, taking second place only to the Maori Anglicans of whom there were 21,738.

As the Young Maori Party had realised a generation earlier, able Maori representation in Parliament was invaluable in furthering the welfare of their people. Now that the Ratana leaders were in control of a powerful unified organisation it was felt that the church should widen its scope and include more work for the material as well as the spiritual benefit of the Maori, and accordingly about 1927 the Ratana Church began to take part in politics. Eruera Tihema Tirikatene – later Sir Eruera – was put forward as a candidate for the Southern Maori electorate in 1928.

Only the casting vote of the returning officer decided the result against him but in August 1932 the death of the successful candidate necessitated a by-election in which Tirikatene won the seat which he retained until his death in 1967. In 1935 the Ratana political movement allied itself with the Labour Party and since then its history has been closely linked with the fortunes of that party.

This alliance was a natural outcome of the special character of the movement which from the start had appealed to the dispossessed, the poor and the uneducated. To the "morehu", as they called themselves, it seemed that the great Maori leaders, Carroll, Ngata, Pomare and Buck, lived in a world apart, a pakeha world, a world of pakeha education, pakeha speech, pakeha ways, a life in which the morehu felt self-conscious and uneasy, and which they scornfully rejected. When such a leader spoke to them they felt that a shadowy pakeha was peering condescendingly over his shoulder. The Ratana movement, on the other hand, gave voice to their own unspoken thoughts. Here were leaders who understood their simple lives, sympathised with them in their misfortunes and appealed to them as kinsfolk.

As a religious and social organisation the Ratana Church continues to play an important part in the lives of its 19,000 adherents to whom it symbolises Maoritanga – but it is a Maoritanga with renewed hope for the future in which the Maori is confidently working out his own salvation in his own way.

The Anglican Church was the first to establish mission stations in New Zealand; it was first in the field and has retained its pre-eminent position as the church with the greatest number of Maori adherents, about 35 per cent of the population. Before and during the wars the majority of Anglican missionaries had made no secret of their sympathies with the Maori people in their troubles and several eminent church leaders had incurred the enmity of the settlers for their outspoken opposition to pakeha aggression.

It is not surprising therefore, that many Maoris whose faith had wavered during those bitter days eventually renewed their allegiance to the faith of their fathers and grandfathers. The eastern area in particular, the Diocese of Waiapu, was a stronghold of Anglicanism. There the great missionary families gave ready help to Maori efforts in education, in improving standards of health and in fostering land development.

By 1925 when a special synod was held to consider the matter, it was felt that the time had come for the Maori people to be under the care of a bishop of their own race. At first it was assumed that a separate diocese would be created but after long discussions and conferences with Maori leaders a compromise was arrived at whereby a Maori suffragan bishop was appointed to act as assistant bishop in the Diocese of Waiapu, but at the same time to have jurisdiction over all Maoris.

The first Bishop of Aotearoa, the Rt. Rev. F. A. Bennett, was consecrated in 1928, a man of outstanding character respected by Maori and pakeha. Born in 1872, the new bishop was of the same generation as Pomare, Ngata and Te Rangihiroa, his mother being of high rank in the Arawa tribe; his father was the son of Dr John Bennett, the first Registrar-General of New Zealand. After receiving his education at St. Stephen's Maori Boys' School in Auckland and at Bishopsdale Theological College, Bennett was ordained deacon in 1896 and priest the following year. His consecration came after many years of devoted mission work among his own people.

On his death, after more than twenty years in high office, Bishop Bennett was succeeded by the Rt. Rev. W. N. Panapa, another former pupil of St. Stephen's College, who was born in 1898 near Dargaville. Through his parents he has affiliations with all the major tribes of Northland and his marriage with a niece of Te Puea Herangi gave him a link with the Waikato people.

Both Roman Catholic and Methodist missions were established in the earliest days of pakeha settlement and the proportion of Maoris belonging to those two churches at the present time is roughly the same as the corresponding proportions of pakehas. Two noteworthy developments in recent years in the Roman Catholic Church have been the ordination of the first Maori priests, and the translation of the Mass into Maori.

On the other hand there are relatively few Maori Presbyterians. Presbyterian missions were not established in the early years and the main Presbyterian centres were well away from the areas of concentrated Maori population. The leeway has never been made up for, apart from those who have embraced purely Maori churches and latterly the Mormon religion, the Maori has shown little tendency to change from one pakeha Christian faith to another. However the Presbyterian Church is actively working among the Maori people at the present day.

The only other religious denomination with significant numbers of Maori adherents is the Church of the Latter Day Saints, the Mormons, who began sending missionaries to the Pacific islands about the middle of last century. A translation of the Book of Mormon into Hawaiian was made in 1856. In New Zealand the Mormon Church, which strongly encourages education, sobriety and conscientious hard work has made considerable advances among the Maori people, and by establishing its Polynesian Cultural Centre in Hawaii it has emphasised the wider unity of all Polynesians, in which the Maori can play a distinguished part.

The outstanding feature which is seen in any survey of spiritual faith among the Maori people today is that, as in ancient times, religion is closely bound in with everyday social life. Religious assemblies bring together people of every walk of life from all over the country and on the marae there is virtually no aspect of Maoritanga which is not discussed.

In an atmosphere of traditional hospitality and courtesies, in surroundings where modern craftsmen have preserved and developed the ancient skills, the Maori of the present generation has the opportunity to discuss the problems of today, problems which he faces with a clearer insight and a hopeful confidence which his ancestors could rarely feel...

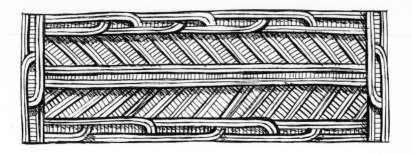

15
Through the Blizzard and the Fire

THE PERIOD OF TWENTY YEARS from 1929 to 1948 was one in which the life of New Zealand was struck by two major disturbances due to forces beyond the control of her people. Like the successive waves of a great storm, the cycle of depression, recovery, war and rehabilitation swept over the country, and it was a New Zealand with a greatly changed outlook which finally emerged.

Both Maori and pakeha felt the impact of the great depression of the 1930s – but in different ways. The pakeha, closely tied to a money economy, was affected more spectacularly as unemployment became widespread; on the other hand those Maoris – and there were many of them – who were already living at subsistence level helped out by seasonal or unskilled work, found that those extra sources of income were no longer available and fell back into real poverty.

Although the Government was prepared to continue with Maori land development schemes, these were seriously hampered by lack of funds, and it seemed as though the high hopes for the future which had been entertained during the previous decade were to prove illusory after all.

But the depression lifted at last and the Labour Government which took office at the beginning of 1936 made a determined effort to make up the leeway. Maori welfare occupied a prominent place in Government plans; as for Social Security in all its aspects, the Maori was given an equal share with the pakeha. In matters of housing and education his need was recognised as being greater and accordingly a proportionately greater effort was made on his behalf. At last, too, there was money available for a rapid expansion of land development; within three years the total acreage of developed Maori land had more than doubled.

It was at this point that the Second World War burst in on a New Zealand which was just beginning to face the future with renewed hope as the clouds of depression rolled away.

Conscription of Maoris was never introduced but the steady stream of volunteers ensured that the Maori Battalion was kept at full strength and active throughout the whole of the conflict. Led by its own Maori officers, appointed with a full appreciation of the traditional principles of leadership, the Battalion made its name as a unit of tough resilient warriors, irresistible in attack and grimly determined in defence. The well-earned award of the Victoria Cross to Second Lieutenant Te Moananui a Kiwa Ngarimu was acclaimed thoughout the whole country and was symbolic of the high esteem in which the Maori Battalion was held by both peoples. Though he lost his life in an action worthy of his greatest ancestors, his name will never be forgotten.

Not only on land but also at sea and in the air, the Maori people shared with their pakeha comrades the hardships and triumphs of six grim years. In the war effort within New

Zealand, too, they gave unstinting support whether in co-operation with pakehas or in independent purely Maori endeavours.

The national consciousness of being New Zealanders together was intensified among both peoples and Maoris throughout the country became increasingly aware of Maori unity in a common cause.

After 1942 the Maori people operated the whole of their own war effort. With a committee of Maori members of Parliament at its head, the organisation worked according to established custom, spreading out through tribal committees to local groups in every part of the country. Tribal loyalties, which had so often defeated attempts at achieving unity in the past, were at last enlisted in a co-ordinated task.

So efficient did the system prove that, at the end of the war, the Department of Maori Affairs took it over as the basis for its own Maori welfare work. Henceforth Maoritanga was to have a wider meaning than it had ever had in practice before.

Psychologically too, the Maori horizon had widened enormously. As with their fathers in 1914-18, the Maori soldiers of the Second World War gained personal insight into the world overseas, but those of the second generation were better educated, better acquainted with pakeha life and so better able to understand the world significance of the events in which they were taking part.

Moreover, on his return to New Zealand the Maori serviceman was able to benefit from Government rehabilitation schemes on the same basis as the pakeha, but with a recognition of his own special needs. Many were thus helped to acquire a trade training which had previously been beyond their reach or not recognised as important.

As with the pakeha ex-servicemen, many did not need or desire rehabilitation assistance. Nevertheless by June 1946, less than a year from the end of the war, nearly a quarter of the Maoris demobilised were receiving educational aid, trade training or farm training, or had been granted loans for farms, housing, business, furniture or tools of trade. Fifteen years later, of a total of 5,352 Maoris demobilised, 4,780 had received assistance of this kind.

Later, in the Korean war and in Malaya, a very high proportion of the New Zealand army was Maori, as also was over a third of the men in the regular forces.

The chance for adventure and travel, opportunities for further education and trade training, a career without the insecurity of unskilled occupations, and above all, the community life, were attractions which helped in varying degrees to influence the young Maori to make his choice.

Although some of the older generation, with memories of the Maori Battalion in their minds, regretted that the Maori troops in Malaya were not formed into a separate unit, it was significant of a change in atmosphere that this was not done. Instead, a policy of complete integration was adopted. Maori and pakeha lived and worked together and came to understand each other the better in the process.

But the obvious success of such a policy had effects which went far beyond the New Zealand troops. In a world where racial conflict looms large, the sight of New Zealand soldiers, pakeha and Maori, working in full co-operation under officers of either group was clear proof to the Asian people that New Zealand's wish for racial harmony and equality was sincere.

This sincerity was still further demonstrated by the appointment in 1959 of Charles Moihi Bennett as the New Zealand ambassador in Malaya. There was real wisdom both in the decision to appoint a Maori to such a post and in the choice of the man. The new ambassador was a son of Bishop Bennett and a man with a distinguished career in war and peace, for he was a former commanding officer of the Maori Battalion, a university graduate, and one of the first two Maoris to study at Oxford University. The other was Dr I. H. Kawharu, now on the staff of Auckland

University. In his four years of office in Malaya, Bennett's personality and ability were of outstanding value in raising New Zealand's prestige abroad.

In the years which followed the war one fact became increasingly obvious: the pressure of world events had completely re-orientated New Zealand thinking. The pakeha had become much more aware of differences between the way of life here and that in Britain, and more conscious of being a New Zealander than ever before. The bonds with Europe were still strong, but the threat of Japanese invasion had forced on him a realisation that Asia was only a few hours' flying time away and that happenings in that continent could be of vital importance to his future.

So, too, the Maori came to feel the presence of Asia, but for him there was a further deep significance. The people of those Malayan villages and towns where the Maori soldier received a friendly welcome, the students from Thailand and Indonesia in New Zealand schools and universities under the Colombo Plan, were his kinsmen, from whom his ancestors had parted three thousand years before. For centuries Maori and South-East Asian had gone their own ways each knowing nothing of the other's existence, but the wheel had gone full circle and they were meeting again in a world vastly different from that in which their forefathers had lived.

It was not only Maori soldiers who went abroad in the post-war years. The desire to travel, which is so marked a feature of New Zealanders today, is far from being a purely pakeha characteristic, and throughout the whole world Maoris are to be found living and working in other countries or passing through as visitors. Moreover for one in a family who travels overseas a dozen others share his experiences in part and broaden their vision from what he learns.

The Maori is taking his part in the modern world. What is more his widening experience is giving him greater confidence as he realises that much of what he had felt was the pakeha way of life in New Zealand is in fact typical of the way of life of progressive peoples of all races throughout the world.

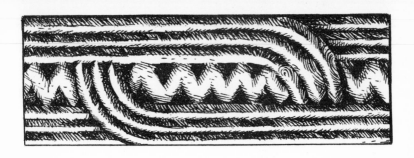

16
The New Migration

IN THE STORY OF THE MAORI PEOPLE after the Second World War, two features are outstanding: the rapid increase in numbers and the movement from the country to the towns.

Between 1945 and 1961 the population grew from 100,000 to 165,000, which was almost double what it had been in 1936, a generation earlier. As the children of the new generation grew up it became obvious that the amount of land available in their home districts was insufficient to support the steadily increasing numbers and it was inevitable that many should leave to seek their living elsewhere.

But before any migration gathers momentum there must be a pull as well as a push. In this case the pressure of population provided the push; the pull came from the towns where labour was in great demand and where wages-money gave opportunities for a fuller life. The outlook of the young people was different from that of earlier generations. For many of them, acquainted with the main stream of New Zealand life through newspapers and radio, that life was not felt to be something apart, something pakeha in which they had no part, but a life which could be theirs too if they were willing to take their opportunity.

There were many problems of adjustment to be faced, difficulties which they did not fully realise until they found themselves away from their familiar environment, but there was a new self-confidence which had been sadly lacking when Ngata, Pomare and Te Rangihiroa began their work.

It was not only the Maoris who moved to the towns. The pakeha was becoming more urbanised too and the proportion of pakeha farmers was decreasing steadily as New Zealand's industry developed; but the noteworthy feature was that, whereas in the past the Maori had remained apart while the pakeha went his own way, now the Maori was sharing in the same developments.

The number of Maoris engaged in primary production – chiefly farming, forestry and mining – remained almost unchanged from 1936 to 1956, but whereas that number formerly had been nearly half of the total, in the latter year it was only one-third. The supply of Maori land is limited and even if all land suitable for development were brought into production it is doubtful if more than five thousand farmers could be settled on the newly developed farms.

Clearly the growth of population has destroyed the old concept that the future of the Maori was on the land. For an increasingly large number of Maoris there will be no land available in the future, even if they wish to become farmers.

Road construction work is nothing new to the Maori for most of the main roads in the North Island were built, either wholly or in part, with Maori labour. Forty years ago it was pick, shovel and wheelbarrow work, but the coming of mechanisation gave an opportunity to gain new skills and in a very short time the Maori bulldozer driver had become a familiar figure wherever there was earth to be moved.

Within an instinctive sensitive touch and an inherited feel for rhythm, he guides and controls the powerful machines as they bite down into deep cuttings or slice away rock and earth on a narrow ledge hundreds of feet up the face of a cliff. The Maori with a machine has power which his ancestors never dreamed of, power to remould the earth.

Driving buses, lorries and locomotives has the same appeal to Maoris, and by 1956 one-tenth of Maori workers were engaged in some occupation connected with transport or communications. But it was industry which absorbed by far the greatest numbers of Maoris in the new age – the qualified as skilled tradesmen, the unqualified as factory hands or labourers.

During the war there had been direction of man-power to industry but the aim was as far as possible to avoid forcing anyone to live away from his home. Nevertheless so great was the need that work was readily available in the cities and larger towns for those who did decide to come to them, and the Maori migration to the towns was well under way before the war ended. Since then there has been no slackening of the flow which, as population has increased, has gathered volume accordingly.

In Northland almost every town, and especially Whangarei, gathered in more Maoris, while the numbers in country areas declined. But the towns of Northland were insufficient to meet the demand. Within the five years from 1956 to 1961, taking into account the natural growth of population through the excess of births over deaths, it appears that nearly a fifth of the Maori people of the seven northern counties left the region altogether. For most of them the end of the journey was Auckland and the nearby districts, where the number of Maoris increased by 9,000 in the same five years.

Similarly, but on a smaller scale, the fringe counties – Raglan, Otorohanga, Waitomo, Coromandel, Thames, Hauraki Plains, Ohinemuri, Tauranga and Opotiki – contributed to the growth of the Maori population of Waipa, Waikato and Whakatane. Power projects and forestry helped Taupo, Rotorua and Whakatane to increase, and in Napier and Hastings, Maori labour for industry was drawn from much of Hawke's Bay province. In the southern half of the island the movement was less spectacular, but everywhere the story was the same; the rural population decreased or barely held its own while the number of Maoris in the towns steadily grew. In 1936, 90 per cent of Maoris lived in the country; in 1956 there were 76 per cent, but within the next five years urbanisation had accelerated so greatly that one in every three was a town-dweller.

The change was a revolutionary one, not only for the Maori people as a whole, but also for the individual facing new problems in unfamiliar conditions.

By far the greater number of those who migrate in search of employment are young. This is true of any migration but it is accentuated by the effects of the rapid increase in the number of Maoris during the past thirty years. Only a quarter of the Maori population is over thirty years of age; nearly half is under fifteen – and the young generation has grown up in the restless post-war world. Among their own people they were under the authority of tribal elders, but once they migrated that restraint – a personal and traditional one – was gone, and in its place they found only the vague and impersonal control of pakeha custom and law.

Maori leaders, well aware of the effects which could follow this profoundly disturbing change, have established in the cities new tribal organisations based on place of residence rather than on kinship, but it takes time for such a radical alteration in the concept of the tribe to become fully accepted.

Meanwhile a small minority, five per cent, has drawn undue attention to itself by lapsing into crime. The proportion of offenders is small, but nevertheless so much greater than that of law-breakers among the pakehas as to cause much concern.

It has been well established, both here and in other countries, that disturbed home life, overcrowding and insecurity of employment are major factors in inducing crime. With many a young Maori all three of these factors operate. Uprooted from his life in familiar surroundings, far too often he finds himself in town, lonely among strangers or living with other Maoris in an overcrowded dwelling. As for employment, he often finds that conditions of work are so different from what he is accustomed to that he drifts from job to job for years before settling down – if he settles down at all.

Moreover a Maori of high intelligence will often discover that lack of familiarity with pakeha modes of life and inability to express himself fluently in English will debar him from the type of work for which he is otherwise suited, and he drifts into purely repetitive work. To a man or youth of alert mind such work can bring only mental stagnation and boredom coupled with a sense of frustration, whether he is Maori or pakeha.

The problem of crime in any society is a complex one, as both material and psychological factors are involved. The Maori people have shown that under the guidance of their own leaders they could face up to and overcome psychological difficulties of adjustment in the past and there is no reason to doubt that in the future they will be equally successful.

But the psychological and the material in the present situation are closely interwoven. The Maori who through lack of sufficient education is forced to accept uncongenial work is all too frequently not only psychologically unsettled but is also chronically short of money. He changes his job often, is unemployed for a while at each change, and the future is so unsure that he spends money while he has it for there is little incentive to save.

However it is not only the Maori in this situation who finds it difficult to cope with managing his money affairs.

Maori traditions of communal life and hospitality made no virtue of individual saving, and from his first acquaintance with money the Maori came to regard it as valuable only in so far as it could be spent on what was wanted at the time.

Generosity to relatives and friends was taken for granted. The stereotype of the kind of pakeha which he disliked was the man who was aloof and suspicious, always thinking about making money which he appeared to regard not as a means to an end but as an end in itself, and who never gave away anything without receiving money in exchange.

It is no wonder therefore that many Maoris still fail to grasp the full significance of the money system and find themselves caught up in a financial tangle through buying on hire-purchase or other forms of time-payment. But shortage of money leads inevitably to poor housing and overcrowding. Maoris coming to the city often found that the only accommodation which they could afford was in the more decadent areas, not slums perhaps by overseas standards, but nevertheless sadly lacking in modern amenities. In such conditions cleanliness was almost impossible, unhealthy surroundings and overcrowding bred disease, and the opportunity to become acquainted with normal pakeha life and to meet pakehas on terms of equality was almost negligible.

It is a credit to many Maori families that they had the determination to rise above their surroundings and by careful management of their finances were able eventually to move to better houses in the suburbs.

But the dice was heavily loaded against them and for many others the problem went round in a circle. Lack of money led to poor housing, poor housing slowed down full integration into New Zealand life, and this in turn kept incomes low. Unless the circle could be broken, there was no hope for improvement.

By 1960 it had become increasingly clear that the problems caused by the new developments among the Maori people could not be expected to solve themselves without outside assistance, and it was realised that immediate action was essential. In that year, the Acting Secretary for Maori Affairs, Mr J. K. Hunn, presented to Parliament a comprehensive survey of the situation of the Maori people together with far-reaching suggestions for improvements.

The response from Parliament was immediate, and the spontaneous willingness to help of the pakeha section of the community left no doubt that the welfare of the Maori was felt to be the responsibility of all.

To the Maori himself, the Hunn Report was a challenge, and in that spirit it was taken up.

17
Education and Unity

MANY OF THE RECOMMENDATIONS of the Hunn Report were ones in which the initiative lay with Parliament, but in one field in particular there was an opportunity for the immediate active co-operation of the Maori people themselves – that of education.

The educational changes introduced into the Maori schools in the 1930s, whereby Maori culture became part of the curriculum and the school itself became much more closely bound up with the life of the community, were undoubtedly desirable, but the whole picture of Maori education had substantially altered a generation later.

In 1930 nearly half the Maori children attending primary school were taught in their own Maori schools; by 1958 the proportion had reduced to barely one-third. This was a natural consequence of the migration away from predominantly Maori areas, but the important result was that the great majority of children were receiving exactly the same education as pakehas in the same state primary schools.

Apart from the 500 pupils in the church boarding schools, other Maoris desiring secondary education in 1930 went to state schools, but scarcely one third of the Maoris who passed Form II received secondary schooling at all. Most of them lived too far away from such schools, and even though a number of Government Maori scholarships were available, boarding accommodation was very limited.

By starting Maori District High Schools in 1941 in remoter areas, the Government gave an opportunity for secondary education to many who would otherwise have had none, and by 1958, with the general school-leaving age fixed at 15, most Maoris were continuing their schooling for at least one high school year, and one in three was still at school at the age of 16, a proportion little different from that of the pakeha. The Maori private schools were by that time educating nearly 1,000 pupils, which by then was less than one-sixth of the total.

As for higher education, instead of the mere handful attending University in 1930, there were 89 Maori students in 1958, including 14 taking courses at the Agricultural Colleges.

It is clear that in one generation there had been a marked advance. Secondary education had been made available to far more Maoris than before, and many more were in fact taking advantage of their opportunity. But for the Maori to be in the same position educationally as the pakeha, much larger numbers should remain in the higher secondary forms and continue their studies at University. In Forms IV and V there was little difference between the proportion of Maoris and pakehas who remained at school, but at the end of the Form V year came a sudden change. Nearly half the pakeha pupils in Form V stayed at school for another year; only one in 11 Maoris did the same.

Why did so many Maoris leave school after Form V? One reason is that their age in that form was on the average a year older than that of pakehas, so that the Maori who left was actually the same age as the pakeha – but a year behind in school-work.

Carefully conducted intelligence testing of both groups shows that there is no real difference in mental ability between them, and the main reasons for this educational lag appear to be home backgrounds offering little encouragement to study, a late start in schooling coupled with further delay in becoming familiar with the English language, and a psychological lack of adjustment to educational methods which are suited to the pakeha, but not always to the Maori.

Yet another factor brought about the final decision to leave school in many cases – lack of finance. The average Maori's income was £200 less than that of the pakeha; the extra £200 a year can make a vast difference in standards of living, and for many Maori parents the decision that they made was exactly the same as that of pakehas in the same financial position. They felt that they could no longer afford to keep a boy at school when he was old and strong enough to earn a man's wage.

All of these handicaps to Maori higher education were considered in the Hunn Report, and recommendations for improvements were made.

Special training for teachers to help Maori pupils to cope with their particular problems; greater educational guidance for pupils entering secondary schools, and vocational guidance later; the establishment of more kindergartens and play-centres in Maori areas; the approach to parents by Maori Welfare Officers to encourage able pupils to stay longer at school; and the setting up of a Maori Education Foundation to provide increased finance for higher education: all were envisaged in the report.

After years of discussion on the marae, and repeated approaches to unresponsive governments, Maori leaders welcomed the reforms of the 1930s; but it was not until the Hunn Report was presented a generation later that they could feel that a real attempt had been made to understand

and grapple with the problems of Maori education.

In particular, the concept of the Maori Education Foundation captured the imagination through its nation-wide scope and its far-reaching possibilities for the future.

In 1961 the Foundation was established by Act of Parliament, and the Government made an initial allocation of £125,000 to its funds; by May the following year subsidised donations had raised the total to almost £400,000.

The fact that more than half of the money collected was from the Maori people themselves showed that they recognised the worth of the Foundation's aims and were prepared to support it wholeheartedly. A Board of Trustees, on which Maori organisations were represented, was set up and at all levels from kindergarten and play-centre to postgraduate research the assistance of the Foundation became available.

Its guiding principle was that every Maori child should be given the opportunity for a full education along the lines for which he was best suited, and to the limits of his ability.

The two Maori organisations represented on the Maori Education Foundation were the New Zealand Maori Council and the Maori Welfare league.

In 1945 the Maori Social and Economic Advancement Act, for promoting the health and general well-being of the Maori people, called on the Maoris themselves to set up executives and committees to control and direct their own communities in accordance with the ideals of good citizenship.

The essential feature was that standards were not being imposed on the Maori from without; he was to set his own standards and enforce them himself. To this end Maori Wardens were appointed with powers to ensure orderly behaviour within their own districts.

The structure of tribal districts and committees grew directly out of the organisation of the Maori war effort which had proved so efficient during the previous three years. By 1961 there were 84 districts and 495 committee areas.

In 1952 a further advance was made by the Maori people: in each Maori Land District delegates from the tribal districts formed District Councils to discuss such problems as affected the whole region. But there was still a final step to take: a national federation of the District Councils.

After several years of discussion among Maori leaders, of whom Major Reiwhati Vercoe of the Arawa federation was the driving force, plans and constitution for such a dominion council were gradually worked out, and in 1961 the Government agreed to its establishment and official recognition as a responsible organisation representing the whole Maori people.

On 28 June 1962 the historic first meeting of the New Zealand Council of Tribal Executives was held, with Sir Turi Carroll as its first President.

Sir Turi Carroll, born in 1890 near Wairoa and educated at Wanganui Collegiate School, Te Aute College and Canterbury Agricultural College, had played a full part in the life of the community and worthily deserved his knighthood in 1962. In public affairs, both of the Maori and the pakeha, his interests and understanding were far-reaching, well fitting him for the responsibilities of the office of President.

The twenty-four council members represented the eight district councils: Tokerau (Northland), Auckland, Waikato-Maniopoto, Waiariki (Rotorua), Tairawhiti (East Coast), Ikara (Hawke's Bay and Wellington), Aotea (Western) and South Island. For the first time all the tribes of New Zealand were united, descendants of all the canoes could speak on the one marae, and the dream of the great leaders of the Maori people 60 years before had at last come true.

The New Zealand Council of Tribal Executives was the crowning achievement in unifying the Maori people, but from the time of the Second World War it had become clear that the spirit of unity was in the air. It was no blind un-reasoning nationalism, challenging the pakeha. Rather it was a challenge to the Maori people themselves to talk over their own problems on the marae, to discuss them constructively at the conference table and to pursue actively all that would promote Maori welfare. The key-note of relations with the pakeha was co-operation.

The Maori Women's Welfare League occupied itself largely with health, housing and education, but no topic which came within the all-embracing scope of welfare was excluded from discussion. The annual conferences brought together representatives of branches from over the whole country. Pakeha members were welcome, but the League remained essentially Maori.

Young Leaders' Conferences, too, both regional and national, gave opportunities for those of the younger generation to present their views, for the limiting age of the young leaders was set at 35. To these conferences a small group of older people was invited but they met in a room apart so that the younger people should not feel overshadowed by their elders. At the same time their experience and knowledge were available if desired.

The development of these conferences owes much to the foresight of Sir Apirana Ngata, who from his own experience with the Young Maori Party fully realised the truth that the young people of today are the leaders of the nation tomorrow.

With Professor Belshaw's assistance he organised the first conference in 1939, and the experience gained there not only showed the potential value of such meetings but also was of great help in future planning.

In 1960 the Auckland University Adult Education Centre, later known as the Department of University Extension, organised a conference of representatives from the whole country. The enthusiasm of Mr S. R. Morrison, director of the department, was reflected in the vigorous discussion during the conference of 1960 and in the regional ones which followed. It was clear that young Maoris had plans for the future and, were prepared to state their views.

The Maori is no longer at the cross-roads. His way lies clear before him and with the initiative, enthusiasm and vigour of the young he is advancing beside the pakeha along the road to the future. With him he is taking all that is best in his ancient culture, for his ancestry means much to him. Even those whose share of Maori blood is slight are proud to declare themselves Maori and identify themselves with the achievements of their people.

The pakeha influence on the Maori for over a century and a half has been profound, but the Maori in his turn has influenced the New Zealand pakeha too, often far more deeply than he realises.

Problems still remain, but none are beyond solution, and both peoples are meeting them with mutual goodwill and a determination that, whatever the future may hold, the ideals of New Zealand as a land of equal opportunities for both races and harmony among its peoples shall remain undimmed.

TIME CHART

(All dates before 1769 must be regarded as approximate only.)

2000–1600 B.C.	Expansion of the Chinese Empire. Polynesian ancestors left Asia.
1000 B.C.	Melanesia settled.
750–500 B.C.	Western Polynesia settled.
200 B.C.	Eastern Polynesia settled.
950 A.D.	First settlement in New Zealand (Kupe & Rakaihautu).
1150	Toi & Whatonga arrived in New Zealand.
1350	Arrival of "The Fleet".
1550	Extinction of the moa.
1769	Captain Cook's first visit.
1814	Arrival of the missionaries.
1840	Treaty of Waitangi.
1853	Te Aute College founded.
1858	Potatau Te Wherowhero elected King.
1860–61	War in Taranaki.
1863–64	War in the Waikato.
1865	Maori Land Court established.
1868	First Maori Members of Parliament.
1891	Te Aute College Students' Association founded. (Young Maori Party.)
1893	First Maori University graduate.
1900	Public Health and Maori Councils Act.
1914–18	First World War.
1918	Ratana's mission began.
1926	Royal Commission on causes of Taranaki Wars.
1928	First Bishop of Aotearoa consecrated.
1929	Native Land and Settlement Act.
1939–45	Second World War.
1955	First New Zealand troops sent to assist Malaya.
1959	First Maori appointed New Zealand High Commissioner overseas.
1960	Hunn Report.
1961	Maori Education Foundation established.
1962	First meeting of New Zealand Council of Tribal Executives.

Short Bibliography of Major Sources

BEAGLEHOLE, J. C. (Ed.). *The Journals of Captain Cook on his Voyage of Discovery*, Vol. 1 C.U.P. for the Hakluyt Society. 1955.

BEST, E. *The Maori As He Was*. Wellington. Govt. Printer. 1952.

BUCK, SIR P. *The Coming of the Maori*. Wellington. Whitcombe & Tombs. 1949. *Vikings of the Sunrise*. Christchurch. Whitcombe & Tombs. 1954.

CODY, J. F. *Man of Two Worlds*. Wellington. A. H. & A. W. Reed. 1953.

CONDLIFFE, J. B. *New Zealand in the Making* – 2nd. Edit. London. Allen & Unwin. 1959.

DUFF, R. D. *The Moa-Hunter Period of Maori Culture* – 2nd. Edit. Wellington. Govt. Printer. 1956.

ELDER, J. R. (Ed.). *Letters and Journals of Samuel Marsden*. 1932. *Marsden's Lieutenants*. 1934.

FIRTH, R. W. *Economics of the New Zealand Maori* – 2nd. Edit. Wellington. Govt. Printer. 1959.

GOLSON, J. (Ed.). *Polynesian Navigation*. Wellington. The Polynesian Society. 1962.

GORST, SIR J. E. *The Maori King* (Ed. K. Sinclair), Hamilton. Paul's Book Arcade. 1959.

GREY, SIR G. *Polynesian Mythology and Ancient Traditional History of the Maori*. Christchurch. Whitcombe & Tombs. 1956.

HENDERSON, J. McL. *Ratana*. Wellington. The Polynesian Society (Inc.). 1963.

HUNN, J. K. *Report on Department of Maori Affairs*. Wellington. Govt. Printer. 1961.

KEESING, F. M. *The Changing Maori*. Wellington. Board of Maori Ethnological Research. 1928.

NGATA, SIR A. T. *The Treaty of Waitangi*. (In Maori). Republished 1963 in English (translated by M. R. Jones) Maori Purposes Fund Board. 1922.

OLIVER, W. H. *The Story of New Zealand*. London. Faber. 1960.

PRICE, A. G. *White Settlers and Native Peoples*. C.U.P. Published in Australia by Georgian House Pty. 1949.

RICKARD, L. S. *Tamihana the Kingmaker*. Wellington. A. H. & A. W. Reed. 1963.

RUTHERFORD, J. *The Treaty of Waitangi and the Acquisition of British Sovereignty in New Zealand*. 1949.

SHARP, A. *Ancient Voyagers in the Pacific*. Penguin Books. 1957.

·SINCLAIR, K. A. *The Origins of the Maori Wars*. Wellington. N.Z. University Press. 1957. *A History of New Zealand*. Penguin Books. 1959.

SUGGS, R. C. *The Island Civilizations of Polynesia*. New York. Mentor Books. 1960.

SUTHERLAND, I. L. G. (Ed.). *The Maori People Today*. N.Z. Council for Educational Research. 1940.

WOOD, F. L. W. *This New Zealand*. Hamilton. Paul's Book Arcade. 1952.

The periodicals, *Journal of the Polynesian Society, Education,* and *Te Ao Hou,* contain many articles from which useful information may be obtained.

GLOSSARY

Ahu – Original meaning: a heap or mound. Although in the Pacific islands the ahu developed into a stone altar-platform in a temple-enclosure, in New Zealand, where it was called tua-ahu, it generally consisted of a roughly-built shrine of stones in a secluded place. When situated in a village it took the form of a wooden post in a sacred enclosure which only the priest could enter. *See* MARAE.

Ariki – A chief of the highest rank. As a title it could be applied only to the eldest son in the senior family of the tribe.

Ati – Prefix to a tribal name. *See* NGAI.

Australoid – The human type to which the aborigines of Australia belong.

Breadfruit – A tropical tree which grows up to 50 feet high. The fruit, as large as a melon, contains a starchy pulp which when roasted is similar to bread.

Caucasian – The somewhat broadly defined human type which includes the peoples of Europe.

Flax (harakeke) – *Phormium tenax,* a plant of the lily family with long fibrous leaves used by the Maori for weaving and rope-making. Rope and sacking are still manufactured from flax, which was one of New Zealand's earliest exports. It is not botanically related to European flax.

Haka – A vigorous posture dance by a group of men under a leader. Although the haka was strictly a peaceful demonstration, the term is now usually applied to all men's group dances with words, thus including war dances.

Hapu – A sub-tribe, a section of a larger tribe under its own chief.

Hauhau – A member of the Pai Marire religion. *See* PAI MARIRE.

Iwi – A nation or people. The term was applied to a tribe.

Kainga – Dwelling-place or unfortified village. Originally meant an encampment. The word is derived from KA (to burn) and signified a place where a fire burned.

Kauri – *Agathis australis,* a coniferous tree which grows up to 150 feet or more in height, and provides an excellent timber for building and joinery, owing to its being strong, straight-grained, easily-worked and free from knots. Digging gum from the ground where ancient kauri forests had been was a profitable occupation until recent years, for it was in keen demand for manufacturing varnishes and linoleum. It is found growing naturally only in New Zealand from North Cape to Kawhia and Maketu, but related species grow elsewhere.

Kumara – *Ipomoea batatas,* the sweet potato, belonging to the convolvulus family, which appears to have originated in South America, but became a major cultivated food-plant throughout Polynesia.

153

Kuri – The Polynesian dog. It was a small short-legged type, with a pointed nose and bushy tail. Brought to New Zealand by the Moa-hunter Maoris, it was for centuries a highly-prized possession of chiefs, but is now extinct.

Mana – Personal prestige and authority. The *mana* of a chief was inherited, but could be still further increased by his wise and capable administration of the tribe.

Mangai – The usual meaning is *mouth*. As a title applied to Tahupotiki Wiremu Ratana, founder of the Ratana Church, the significance is that of prophet in the Biblical sense, the speaker of the words of God.

Maori – The original meaning of the word was *usual* or *normal*. Hence it was applied to themselves by the Polynesians of New Zealand to distinguish themselves from the strange and unusual European people. In this sense it has been used from about 1830.

Maoritanga – The modern meaning is the consciousness of being Maori and so inheriting the Maori tradition. Hence it is extended to include all that is traditionally Maori.

Marae – The village meeting-ground on which discussions are held. In the other Pacific islands the *marae* became closely associated with the religious rites of the *ahu* but in New Zealand it remained secular.

Melanesia – The island groups of New Guinea, Solomon Islands, New Hebrides and New Caledonia. Fiji is usually included also, but in many respects it is a fringe area which has many links with Polynesia.

Moa – Various species of wingless birds found only in New Zealand and now extinct. The largest types, which stood up to 12 ft. in height, had apparently died out before the earliest Moa-hunting Maoris arrived. The species hunted by the Polynesian settlers was Euryapteryx, about five feet high.

Mongoloid – The human type to which the Chinese people belong.

Negroid – The human type which includes the African Negro.

Niu – A pole round which the Hauhaus conducted their religious ceremonies. This word was usually applied to small sticks used in foretelling the future, but in the rest of Polynesia it means *coconut-palm*.

Nga – The (plural).

Ngai, Ngati, Ati – Prefixes meaning *tribe,* literally *descendants.*

Pa – A fortified place. From the verb PA (to obstruct).

Pai Marire – The fanatical religion of the Hauhaus, founded by Te Ua in 1862. The name means *good and peaceful!*

Pakeha – A person of predominantly European descent.

Poi – A light ball, often of bulrush leaves (Raupo) with an attached string. In women's dances poi balls are twirled rhythmically in time with a song.

Polynesia – The islands of the eastern Pacific Ocean, included within a triangle formed by New Zealand, Easter Island and Hawaii.

Rangatira – A tribal chief.

Ringatu – The religion founded by Te Kooti Rikirangi in 1868. The name means *uplifted hand*.

Tangi – Ceremonial weeping and lamentation. Now used in a wider sense to mean the whole procedure of a funeral gathering at which the local people may be hosts to considerable numbers of visitors from other districts.

Tapu – Any form of spiritual restriction. A chief was personally *tapu* with an inherited sacredness, extending also to his possessions which would accordingly never be touched by a commoner. Other forms of *tapu* were measures of hygiene enforced through religious awe, for example the death *tapu*, whereby a house in which a death had occurred would never again be lived in.

Taro – A large-leafed food-plant cultivated throughout tropical and sub-tropical regions for its starchy corm.

Taurekareka – A slave, usually a captive taken in battle. The taurekareka had no human rights whatever, and once a chief had become a captive and slave his mana was lost for ever, even though he might later escape.

Te – The (singular).

Tohunga – An expert. The term was usually used of priests, but could be applied also to a skilled craftsman. The word is derived from TOHU (a mark or sign), and so meant an outstanding person.

Tua-ahu – *See* AHU.

Tukutuku – Decorative lattice-work in wall panels.

Tutua – The lowest rank of free men in Maori society.

Urukehu – A fair-skinned type of Maori with bronze-red hair. People of this type were not often found, but had been known among the Maori people from long before the European discovery of New Zealand.

Utu – Price, reward or recompense. The term was applied to recognised punishment, such as the unresisted plundering of a minor offender's possessions, and also to the killing of a member of another tribe, whether innocent or guilty, as revenge for a murder committed by someone from that tribe.

Waka – A canoe. It was also used to denote a tribe, i.e., those who traced their descent from the crew of a particular canoe.

Whare Whakairo – A carved and adorned meeting-house. There is some doubt as to whether the building of special meeting-houses is a custom of very long standing, but at the present time the meeting-house is the focal point of a Maori community and a visible indication of strong tribal pride.

Yam – A tropical climbing plant, cultivated for its tuberous roots, which are used in the same way as potatoes.

No. 1: A Maori rafter pattern named "Ngutu Kaka".

These patterns form an important part of Maori decorative art. They are mainly designs painted on the rafters of the larger meeting houses in black and white or in red, black and white. It is claimed that the patterns are based on natural forms and the names would appear to confirm this. Some students, however, think the artists drew designs which pleased their aesthetic tastes and then chose the names.

The name "Ngutu Kaka" means the beak of the kaka, a brown parrot native to New Zealand. The interlocking crescents of the design certainly suggest this.

There is a shrub called ngutu-kaka for the same reason, that is, its red flowers are like parrots' beaks. It would seem that the design owes more to this flower than to the actual bird's beak as the design looks quite like a mass of the flowers. In addition, the small circles within the crescents suggest the seeds of the plant.

This design was first recorded on the east coast, in the area occupied by the Ngati Porou tribe.

No. 2: A Maori rafter pattern, a development of the design known as "Kowhai" and probably based on the flower of the same name.

No. 3: A Maori rafter pattern, a variant of the design known as "Mangopare" and said to be based on the head of a hammer-headed shark. This design recorded by the artist in a Ngati Porou meeting house.

No. 4: This Maori wood carving design is called "Maui" and is said to be based on two interlocking fish hooks. Maui was the legendary hero who was said to have caught New Zealand on his fish hook and hauled it from the depths of the ocean. The Maori name for the North Island is Te Ika-a-Maui – The Fish of Maui. This design is frequently carved as a surface decoration on the figures which form the wall slabs of the more elaborate meeting houses. It is favoured for hip and shoulder decoration as it emphasises the roundness of these parts of the basic carved figure.

No. 5: A Maori wood-carving design, used as surface decoration on large figures or on small articles. This design is called "Rauponga", meaning tree-fern frond.

No. 6: A close view of the notch-and-ridge carving used so frequently in surface decoration. The ridges are called "haehae" and the notches "pakati". Other types of surface decoration are considerably more complicated.

No. 7: A carving of a mythological sea monster called "Marakihau". The Marakihau were said to have had tubular tongues through which they sucked fish and even canoes – crew and all. The one drawn has a fish-like tail and is in the act of drawing a fish into its tongue. This is based on a Bay of Plenty carving.

No. 8: A Taranaki carving, based on an "epa" or store-house panel. The carved figures of this district are remarkable for their twisted forms and serpentine bodies. Note the interlocked arm and leg and the arm which goes through the mouth and back to join the body. Remarkable examples of this style of carving have been recovered from swamps in the Waitara district of Taranaki and may be seen in the New Plymouth Museum.

No. 9: A design of the type often found on the threshold of meeting houses. It features a central full-faced head in the style known as "Wheku" and is flanked by inward-facing heads in profile known as "Manaia". The Manaia is one of the most frequently used forms of carving and has countless variations. It is used on the largest carvings and even on small pieces of ornament such as combs and pendants.

No. 10: A hand club known as "Wahaika", usually made of whalebone. Clubs of this kind made of wood were used more as an orator's baton than as a weapon.

INDEX

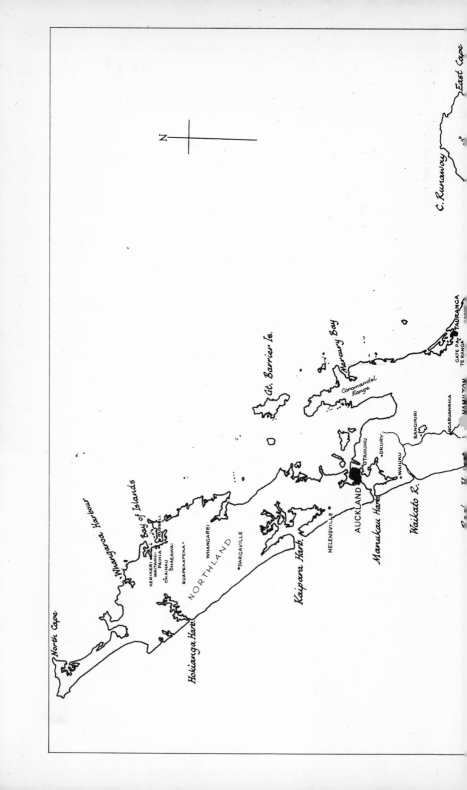